How to Get
Free
PR

For Your Business & Be PAID For It

Helen Dewdney
The Complaining Cow

Copyright © 2024 Helen Dewdney

The Complaining Cow
Trademark of Helen Dewdney

https://www.thecomplainingcow.co.uk

The right of Helen Dewdney to be identified as the author of this work has been asserted in accordance with the Copyright, Designs and Patents Act 1988.

All rights reserved. No part of this publication may be reproduced, stored in a retrieval system, or transmitted, in any form or by any means, electronic, mechanical, photocopying, recording or otherwise, except as permitted by the UK Copyright, Designs and Patents Act 1988, without the prior permission of the publisher.

Although the author and publisher have made every effort to ensure that the information in this book was correct at going to press, the author and publisher do not assume and hereby disclaim any liability to any party for any loss, damage, or disruption caused by errors or omissions, whether such errors or omissions result from negligence, accident, or any other cause. If professional advice or other expert assistance is required, the services of a competent professional should be sought.

Book typesetting and cover design *StudioXB.com*

ISBN 9780993070464

Dedicated to my teenage son Oliver
who would never do any of this
in a month of Sundays!

Contents

Foreword—Jeremy Vine vii

Introduction 1

CHAPTER 1 Starting to get publicity in mainstream media 3

CHAPTER 2 Prepare for your coverage 51

CHAPTER 3 At the event 59

CHAPTER 4 Getting paid 71

CHAPTER 5 After your appearances 77

CHAPTER 6 Building your media contact list 91

CHAPTER 7 Sending out press releases 95

CHAPTER 8 Boost your profile outside of traditional media 111

CHAPTER 9 Write yourself and get your name out there 131

CHAPTER 10 Performing at your best so you are asked back! 135

CHAPTER 11 Be true to yourself 143

Glossary 147

References 153

Acknowledgements 175

Foreword
Jeremy Vine

It was the buggy. My wife had been to collect it from—let's say, in classic BBC style—the largest outlet of a well-known high street purveyor of prams. The trip was thirty miles, to Staines (the home of Ali G). She then returned to Hammersmith (home of the Vine family).

When she got back to our place, she found they had sold us the wrong buggy; it was not a model that would fit in our car. I was at work. Rachel had parked carefully, got out of the car, extracted the box from the boot, heaved it indoors despite being eight months pregnant and sliced the cardboard lid apart with a Stanley knife. She immediately saw the firm's error.

I got home from work and was cross. She calmed me down. It was all fine. She had called the store about the error and been assured the correct buggy was in stock. She asked them to deliver but they said, "It would be better if you collected it." To me that seemed unfair—another thirty-mile round trip, more petrol and more precious time—but my wife is a patient soul.

The following night I arrived home to discover her in tears. She had repacked the first buggy, reloaded the car and re-driven to Staines. A distracted worker with no knowledge of the case had eventually found her the buggy replacement while chewing gum. Rachel loaded the box in the boot and drove it home, cut it open with the very same Stanley knife—and discovered it was broken. A piece of hard plastic in the mount had sheared off and a wheel was loose.

I came home and asked her what the tears were for and she said those four words: "It was the buggy." She had contemplated ringing the store and complaining, but what if they just said, "Come a third time and we'll sort it out?" It was clear that the company did not really care. The thought of driving all that way to collect another buggy would send her over the edge.

At this point, trying desperately to make myself useful, I remembered a guest who had appeared on my Radio 2 show the previous Monday. It was hard to forget her—Helen Dewdney had insisted we style her "The Complaining Cow" on air; you wouldn't disobey someone with that kind of rider. She had taken listener calls on various letdowns by big companies. She was, of course, full of great advice. Big companies are hard to penetrate. "Be prepared to go public," she said. "Never be rude." But the thing I remembered most clearly was this:

You need to attract the attention of the person at the top. One way is a poem.

So I sat down that night and typed what I considered to be the most polite-angry poem in the history of English literature.

> *All we wanted was a decent pram*
> *To wheel around our lovely baby when she appears;*
> *First you sent us the wrong one,*
> *Then a broken one,*
> *And made my wife burst into tears.*
>
> *Your delivery people told us*
> *They could not collect the wrong pram;*
> *I guess they were in bed.*
> *So you asked my eight months pregnant wife*
> *To do the driving instead.*
>
> *Rachel drove forty miles for you,*
> *Because you are a lazy and selfish firm.*
> *You swapped the wrong pram*
> *For a broken one;*
> *She only discovered when she got home.*
>
> *The pram will now be dropped with us*
> *On the day the baby is due—*
> *That's what you told my wife.*
> *It's lucky you're not delivering our child,*
> *Because it would never arrive.*

I found out the name of the chief executive and posted the poem. We waited for a response.

Foreword

Before I tell you what happened next, I should say that I reckon you'll have wondered why I'm writing the foreword to this book. I'm a reporter and reporters hate PR, right? Sure, I've interviewed Helen scores of times over the years and we've always got on well. I like her style and I like her life tips. But *Public Relations?* Is that what this is about? What would I know about PR? I mean, somebody once said: "Journalism is all the news they don't want you to hear. The rest is advertising."

You'd expect me to be wary of endorsing a book about *How To Get Yourself On A Radio Show*. Every day we have at least a dozen emails from people who are lobbying for a person or a product or a book; often, lobbying very badly. They say "Our client would love to be on *Radio Three*," or "has always wanted to meet Jeremy Vince." The stories are regularly pap—the lonely quantum physics professor who has finally got in the *Daily Mail* with a story about his "formula for a perfect burger" now thinks he can get on the radio with a "formula for the perfect beach"—*sorry mate, the burger story was rubbish and this one is too and you know it.* We once got done by a brilliant PR firm who got a number of mums to set up a "Campaign for Happy Endings," apparently because they were upset by the unfortunate outcome of the new Lemony Snicket book. Only a week after the item aired did the penny drop. The mums were *promoting* Lemony, not criticising him. Yeah, yeah, I thought, well done. You cheated your way on air. I still get cross when I'm in a bookshop and see a Snicket. I'd call that a backfire.

But that's not what Helen is writing about or suggesting here. She's not doing the devious PR stuff, but rather making wholly honest and interesting suggestions about how you reach out—I can hardly object to her suggestion that it might be a good idea to work out who you're speaking to before you ring them; what the story is; what your expertise is. All good! There are no dark arts in here because dark arts don't work.

Two days after I sent the poem, there was a knock at our front door. Rachel opened it to see a middle-aged man in a suit. A regional manager for the baby gear firm arrived with a stuffed teddy, the correct buggy, chocolates and flowers. He could not have been nicer. He even handed over a card signed by all the staff at the branch where the trouble had started. I got home and thought: "Next time Helen asks me for something, I'm going to say yes."

So here I am.

Introduction

As always, thanks first and foremost to my long-suffering friend, mentor and editor Marcus Williamson for the suggestions, the editing of what seemed like hundreds of versions and proof reading. Back in 2012 I started *The Complaining Cow* blog, sharing stories of tackling companies with poor customer service. It resulted in the publishing of two best-selling consumer advice books and lots of media coverage. Having gained recognition for my expertise and knowledge of consumer matters and complaint handling, I can often be seen and heard in the media, with my no-nonsense direct style. As a credible and authentic expert, I have regularly appeared on around 200 media outlets, including BBC *One Show*, *ITV Tonight*, *BBC Breakfast*, *BBC Morning Live*, documentaries, *Jeremy Vine* on 5 and various programmes on *BBC Radios 2*, *4*, *5*, *Scotland* and *Wales*.

Within months of starting the blog I obtained local media coverage and after a year I was paid to be an 'expert' on *BBC Radio 5*. From there, I started to get regular local, regional and national coverage on radio, newspapers, magazines and TV. Within a few years I was getting paid for it. I've now even pulled away from most unpaid media work. Work in the media is now one of my income streams and gives me PR! So, it has double benefits.

It is possible for anyone to get Public Relations (PR) coverage, often with a little bit of luck. However, for most of us it's a matter of either paying someone to get the coverage or work at it oneself. I haven't ever paid for PR but I have worked hard for it. I have undertaken nearly all of the suggestions in this book. It takes time and effort to build up your contacts, discover and take advantage of the opportunities out there and get known as the expert and the 'go to' person for the media to get that PR. This in turn can lead to paid work, giving you income as well as free PR.

I have always had a passion for fighting injustice. I started complaining to companies that didn't keep to agreements or broke consumer law, from the age of 11!

Now an established consumer champion, I also support small businesses to develop their terms and conditions and challenge and support companies to transform and improve their complaint handling through customer insights and perspectives. My unique approach sees customer service through a new lens.

My strong mainstream and social media presence mean that I regularly have the ear of consumers. I know what they want in complaint handling and customer service. I support businesses in focusing on continual improvement with ongoing challenge and support through consultancy, workshops and more and my PR has played a significant part in that success.

Although the title of this book is *How to Get Free PR for Your Business—and Be Paid for It*, it's not truly free, in that it will cost you time and energy. I do also refer to one paid way of getting PR that complements the other ideas but I think it's essential.

Paying someone to do your PR is certainly easier and quicker! However, there are a number of ways you can build up your coverage which a PR person would not do. But only a few are quick wins! You will need to undertake both proactive and reactive activities to get the results you desire. You will need to work out if paying someone to do your PR (and thoroughly check the contract!) is a better option than using your time. There are also a number of tips which help both your PR and other areas of your business too.

There will be wobbles on your PR journey as you build your confidence and experience, but this book will help you with that!

CHAPTER 1

Starting to get publicity in mainstream media

What is PR?

PR is Public Relations, a process of managing communication from you or your company to the public, to influence their perception of you.

When you appear in the media, whether local, regional, national, international, radio, online or TV, that raises your profile. The classic line "No such thing as bad publicity" may or may not be true but it does get your name out there. If you are a business it helps people to get to know you and what you do. People buy from people.

It can be as simple as keeping your audiences up to date with what key figures in your industry or you are doing. When you get noticed for speaking up, you'll be noticed and viewed as a knowledgeable resource.

You can pay for advertorials, which read like articles but are actually an advertisement and have to be labelled as such to abide by the Advertising Standards Authority rules. You can pay for adverts on radio, TV and online. Even paying for Google Adwords is a form of PR. But arguably the best PR is where you are telling a story or sharing your expertise with the public. This can be in the first person or you can be interviewed or provide comment for features.

In the digital era, social media plays a big part in PR too. Influencer marketing, blogs, websites and social media should also form part of your business strategy. You need a holistic approach.

PR is important for any business. It should be part and parcel of any marketing strategy. But it doesn't have to be expensive or in fact cost anything, except time. But be in no doubt, a lot of time. It aids credibility as well as increasing the visibility of your business.

It shows thought leadership and gets you talked about and when others talk about you it's more powerful than you talking about yourself. It's great for brand awareness and trust in it which will increase your overall customer loyalty and therefore sales.

Cheaper than placing adverts which have a clear aim to sell, positive PR is the equivalent of a trustworthy word-of-mouth way of getting your message out there. Ultimately, the media has a bigger reach than you!

A PR person is an individual or an agency who works on your behalf to get the PR for you. Their work involves contacting media outlets and arranging interviews. They have the contacts and know where to look for opportunities that fit, taking away the hard work, time and effort that you would have to spend on getting your own PR! This is sometimes referred to as "Earned PR" because it's all about building trust, credibility and getting people talking about you. It includes mentions in magazines, papers, industry outlets, radio, social media and high website rankings.

The thought of trying to obtain publicity may be daunting. You may feel like you'll never get it. But it is possible! Start small. Get the experience and grow from there. I started with the smallest audience possible in the local free paper for Waltham Forest back in November 2013. It's a long game too and you have to keep at it to retain momentum.

1 Decide why you want PR

Plan your objectives. Decide why you want PR. Is it for brand awareness? To launch a new product or service? To gain new customers? To enter a new market? Is it a mix of these for different reasons? Be as specific as you like. Working out and writing these down will help you determine which of these tips to try first, whom to target, how and when.

Obviously, you can change and adapt as you see what works, what doesn't and how to fit in with other priorities.

Jill Foster, a journalist, says "When people apply to be in a story, I always advise that they go into it with open eyes. Your quote and your picture may be seen across the world so you need to be aware of that. If you want to raise awareness of a cause or charity, then great. But if it's a more personal story, you need to be 100 percent certain that you're comfortable with hundreds of thousands—even millions—of people reading it."

2 Get your mindset in a good place

This may seem strange but it's important to recognise that PR is part of your work. Don't be shy about it. In fact, talk about it as part of your business to people you know and online. For example, Tigz Rice—a photographer—always makes a point of vocalising her goals to as many people as she possibly can! She strongly believes in those six degrees of separation working wonders!

In order to publicise her photography business, she tweeted that she wanted to be on more podcasts. Someone recommended her to the BBC's *The Naked Podcast*, which resulted in her being interviewed naked in a Kings Cross hotel room in January 2020!

Remember, too, that it's not all about you. The messaging you are providing will also be helping people.

> The six degrees of separation theory was an experiment undertaken by American psychologist Stanley Milgram. It demonstrated that on average any two individuals anywhere in the world are separated by just five connections. So this means that you can connect with someone by communicating with one person and from them to another and so on, until the sixth connection.

3 The 7 touch points of marketing

Dr Jeffrey Lant suggested that people need to be "touched" by you seven times before they will buy from you. However, this was before the numerous digital channels that we now have and the analysis tools available. Given the increased number of ways there are for absorbing content, and the amount of content there is, this figure is likely to be much higher. However, you can apply the concept rather than a rule.

A touch point could be hearing you on the radio, reading about you in a newspaper, seeing you on TV, an advert, an email newsletter, a phone call, your logo on a leaflet, etc.

It is the combination of all these things that help raise your profile. So you want to ensure that you work on a variety of outlets!

See also **160 Monitor the effects of coverage**.

4 Read the book and make a plan!

There are a lot of tips in this book! Many of them are actions but you cannot do them all at once. PR is a long game and a combination of steps that you can take to increase your visibility, credibility and ultimately your sales. You won't suddenly be frequently featured on a wide variety of platforms, showing off your expertise.

Read at least this chapter, then **CHAPTER 5 After your appearances**, **CHAPTER 6 Building your media contact list**, **CHAPTER 7 Sending out press releases** and **CHAPTER 8 Boost your profile outside of traditional media** and make notes on which tips you fancy doing the most and write a plan of action.

Start with your objectives and what you want to achieve. Decide on how long you want to spend on PR each day/week, where and what

---

Ensure your objectives are SMART—Specific, Measurable, Achievable, Realistic/Relevant and Timebound (e.g. to respond to 5 press call outs a month, to pitch a story to journalists once a week).

SPECIFIC
Clearly defined

MEASURABLE
Can count your responses

ACHIEVABLE
If you follow the advice in this book you will be able to reach these targets

REALISTIC/RELEVANT
Allow a set time each week to undertake this work ensuring relevant to your business

TIMEBOUND
Dates in place

CHAPTER 1 Starting to get publicity in mainstream media

you are going to work on when. Organise your tasks and time and how you will measure success. Set actions, targets and goals for coverage. Could it be reaching certain outlets, for example, or the number of times you want to be quoted as an expert or a case study?

Be clear on the messages you want to provide and the image you want to portray.

Whilst many of the methods may be part of your marketing strategy, the overall strategy should be different. Marketing is about driving sales, whilst PR is about raising profile which may ultimately lead to sales.

This should all form part of your business strategy.

5 Local press

Start with looking at your local newspaper, if you have one, whether it's a free or paid edition. This was the first piece of printed media I did, an opinion piece in *Waltham Forest News*, back in November 2013, on the importance of complaining effectively about consumer issues. Before I did it, I asked a few people in a Facebook group if a similar activity had been useful for them. Many people said that they had received large numbers of social media 'follows' after they did a piece. I didn't get lots of follows but I did get a few and at this point I didn't have anything to sell, either!

6 Local online press

Don't forget online local press too. Janine McDonald, founder of Clear the Clutter Now, and author of *Clear the Clutter Now: Streamline Your Life by doing Just 3 Things* set up her business just before the Coronavirus lockdown. She contacted a reporter from an online local newspaper asking if he would be interested in covering the story. He was and it then got picked up by three different newspapers.

7 Contact your local radio station

Rhiannon Abbott is the owner of The Epsom Bakehouse. She teaches people to bake bread at home via online classes and a membership club. When she heard that her local BBC Radio station was going to discuss *The Great British Bake Off* show, she phoned them and offered to go on and join the discussion. She then took part in several other shows for the series. As they had her details, she was invited back in subsequent years for follow-ups.

8 Invite the press to events

If you are running an event, contact your local press who are often looking for stories and good pictures.

Diane Ivory, a former Scotland Yard fingerprint expert and Crime Scene Examiner, now runs workshops and events through her company Forensic Minds. She spent a week delivering workshops at a college and invited a local journalist and a photographer to run a piece on her.

See **87** Hold an event.

9 Local free advertising

Sometimes a local paper will offer a free to advertise slot to promote local businesses. Do this where you can, as you may gain more than just new customers.

Linda Gransby owns Memories and Photos. She runs residential craft weekends, a monthly Scrap Box Club and online shop. Her local paper has a free to advertise "What's On" guide where she lists all her photo album and scrapbooking workshops and events.

A BBC researcher saw her ads and asked her to talk about photo and memory preservation and organisation for a slot on local radio. This included being able to give out her contact information, website and social media details.

CHAPTER 1 Starting to get publicity in mainstream media

10 Present local/community radio

This wasn't something I tried at first, although I should have done. I mistakenly thought living in London there weren't any local stations because there were so many big ones serving the capital! But this is a great opportunity for anyone. So, when I was ruing the fact that I never got round to doing a podcast, I thought I'd look again at what was available. I was delighted to then be asked to present *The Complaining Cow Consumer Show* for East London Radio, which for me was the equivalent of doing a podcast without the hassle.

Research what is available in your area and offer to be a guest.

If you think you have an idea for my show, email me! helen@eastlondonradio.org.uk

Also, many radio stations offer training and opportunities for budding presenters. So, offer to present a show or appear as a guest talking about your area of expertise. The audience is, of course, relatively small but a good story on local radio may get picked up elsewhere on other media. If you get your own show you will be able to add "presenter" to your bio.

11 #JournoRequest

On X (formerly Twitter), follow the hashtag *#JournoRequest* daily and you will see requests for a wide variety of journalist enquiries. Maybe "Who eats a box of Liquorice Allsorts every day?" There are always many of these tagged tweets, all the time, every day. Anything from seeking a victim of a particular crime to a request for unusual hobbies, such as collecting bottle tops!

When looking at these, remember that these will not always be work-related. It could be that they are seeking topical stories or case studies. Many will offer to mention a business by name and give a web link, if it is relevant. But don't insist on it!

Dr Clair Burley, an independent Chartered Clinical Psychologist, has gained a lot of success from keeping an eye on this hashtag, with two inclusions in *The Independent*, one in *Style Magazine* and another in *Elle*.

On X, look up *#JournoRequest* & *#PRRequest*.

PAGE 9

If you look once or twice a day for the *#JournoRequest*, keep a note of journalists who look like they're always asking for case studies and topics that might be similar to yours. When you're ready, you could approach them with your idea.

See **20** **Email the journalist**.

12 *#JournoRequest* case study request group

This Facebook group reaches far fewer people than the X (formerly Twitter) hashtag or Lightbulb (See **25** **Facebook Lightbulb group**) and there are very few posts. It may pick up, it may fold!

However, some journalists will post in here looking for case studies as well as elsewhere. The more places you have your eyes for opportunities, the more likely you are to get them!

13 JournoLink

Although this costs money, you can get free emails that request input from professionals in a given field. You do have to pay to reply but sometimes they put their name and/or email address in the blurb. You can then email that person or go to the *#JournoRequest*, find them that way and respond. You could choose to pay if you receive a request that you think is worth the payment.

14 Press Plugs

Press Plugs also costs money, but one week trials are available. Sign up to receive press requests in your selected sectors of interest.

15 Check Instagram

Although not as frequent as *#JournoRequest* on X (formerly Twitter), some

CHAPTER 1 Starting to get publicity in mainstream media

opportunities arise on Instagram. You might see an opportunity to network, be on a podcast or see a call out from a journalist. Business Strategist Linda Scerri, who runs Save Money Make Money, saw a post from a journalist on Instagram asking for people who had any money saving/making stories. Linda got in touch and was then featured in several women's magazines.

16 Editorielle

Depending on which membership you take out, Editorielle provides PR opportunities daily or as they come in and are approved by the team. From a variety of sources such as #JournoRequest and unique direct requests now too. (Journalists submit their requests directly to Editorielle through its website which they then distribute). It filters these and only includes #JournoRequests from verified journalists and established publications, to ensure they're all free editorial opportunities from high calibre outlets. You can get a free trial by emailing *freetrial@editorielle.com*

Roxy King-Clark, a coach, has received several pieces of coverage from Editorielle from giving commentary to being a case study in *Metro*'s "Masks, vaccines and mental health: How Covid has shaped the world".

17 Dot Star Media

Dot Star Media is another service which tracks the #JournoRequests. It says that most alerts are delivered within 30 seconds of the posting. You can select to receive requests from lots of different areas, such as personal finance, shopping, lifestyle, business, commerce etc. It's costly, at £40 a month, but there is a free 14-day trial.

18 Research the outlet

If, for example, you wanted to appear on *You and Yours* on *BBC Radio 4*, listen to some shows before making contact with the team there. Consider the type of subjects they cover, length of time people are on, types of debate, etc, before making your approach.

The same applies to printed media. Research your possible outlets in depth before contacting the relevant editor with your ideas.

Take a look at Readly and PressReader. At the point of publishing there is a one week free trial for Readly and two months for PressReader. The sites both list all the articles from over 7,000 outlets. This means that you can look for a keyword, for example. So, if your area of expertise is speech therapy, you could put "speech therapy" into the search bar and articles mentioning speech therapy will be shown.

You can then dig deeper into which outlets might cover your story where you could offer a different angle and the style in which they write. For example, you may have an outlet that likes 'hacks', such as 10 top tips. So you could do "10 top tips to help your child's speech development at home".

You can also Google one of your topics and click "news" in the search. This will bring up articles on that theme which will give you some idea of outlets which might cover your angle, if you approached them.

Look at who writes for the outlets that you think would work well for you. They all operate in different ways. Some will have a link from the journalist's name to an email address or have a "Meet the team" page with links. Some will have an editor's email address and sometimes you will be able to work out the email format.

For example, *firstname.surname@domain*

Don't use the generic *info@* email address, as this will not get to the right place.

19 Look at frequency

When you're searching previous magazine and newspapers, look for keywords that reflect your expertise. Determine how often an outlet covers the topic. For example, a woman's magazine may cover the menopause in an article every two months. So, you can see that if you've got a different angle or a new case study, there's a chance that they will cover it.

If, however, they covered the subject a year or two ago, you may think they're unlikely to cover it again, but, on the other hand, enough time may have passed for you to provide a different story.

Joe Nutkins runs Dog Training for Essex & Suffolk. She researched what *Vanity Fur*

Magazine had published in previous articles on their digital version by subscribing to it and reading it through. She looked up the relevant person to contact and then messaged, introducing herself, including her experience and qualifications. She asked if they would be interested in her writing an article for them.

Joe included a couple of links to her blogs so they could see how she wrote and suggested she write about Senior Dogs or Dog Fitness. She noticed there hadn't been anything so far covering these topics and that these are both areas in which she specialises.

Joe emailed the Assistant Editor and they asked her to write an article about Senior Dogs for the next issue which had a deadline of 4 weeks later.

20 Email the journalist

Having researched the outlet, personalise a pitch to the appropriate journalist showing that you have read their other articles and outline how you believe you would be a good fit for them. Ask if they would they like to include you in an article.

21 Research journalists and think about whether to typecast them

When you find a journalist, look at the type of stories they cover. Do they only write about one specific area? Have they written about other things? If only once or twice is it possibly because it was an issue close to them or a case study known to them? In which case stick with their main specialism of writing.

Punteha van Terheyden is a very experienced journalist, editor and mentor. She says "When pitching an idea to a freelance journalist, first research the journalist you're pitching. If they write real-life stories, there's not much point sending them something on theatres. If you're sending to a bunch of journalists in one go, focus on strengthening your pitch."

But on the other side, sometimes journalists fancy a change or are seeking to develop their skills. For example, I write about consumer issues. But after about

6 years I started to expand a little and write up individual case studies. The first was for the *Metro* about a single mum's lockdown business coaching people on LinkedIn which let her ditch renting to buy her first home. It is money-related, though, as it was about how Leah grew a business in lockdown. I also wrote about "Pastime to full-time: How the pandemic made us turn our hobbies into main jobs." So, you can see that in my role as a journalist, I would be interested in writing about non-consumer issues but probably still money-related.

22. Undertake research with your ideal client and actual clients

Research your current clients. If you have a Facebook group, for example, ask the members what radio station they listen to, what magazines they read, what programmes they watch, etc. Where does your ideal client hang out? Build and maintain the relationships with journalists there by following the tips and see **18. Research the outlet** above.

23. ResponseSource

Sign up for the ResponseSource week-long free trial. Journalists send requests for case studies/expert comment through the service by email. You can select the sectors of interest to you and you will then receive requests from journalists on those topics. You can then reply with details about how you can help. You receive the emails as they are sent, in real time.

Taking advantage of a two-week free trial, Dalia Hawley, founder of Dalia Botanique, responded to a request and got her brand, products and images included in a piece "Money Matters—Deal of the week" in *Woman's Own*. She also responded to a request for beauty trends and suggested her products to the journalist for *Natural Health Magazine*. Dalia was featured in a paragraph on sustainability in skincare with one of her products, a shampoo bar. To top off the trio she responded to another request and was featured in "Christmas with a Difference" in *Woman and Home* talking about riding long distances on Christmas Day.

CHAPTER 1 Starting to get publicity in mainstream media

24 Go international

Sites such as Help a Reporter Out (HARO) and SourceBottle serve journalists and experts internationally, including the UK. This is similar to **23 Response Source**, above, where journalists send requests for case studies/expert comment through the service by email. It sends three emails a day. You can select some of the sectors of interest to you and will receive requests from journalists on those topics. You can then reply to the journalist through the site. You can pay to upgrade from the basic service.

Qwoted is another international site that lists journalists around the world. You can see requests and also pitch. You can set up a profile with hashtags so outlets can search for you, too.

Mangla Sachdev is the founder of Expat Business in a Bag, which is for expats, military spouses and digital nomads. She is originally from London, lived in Melbourne, Malaysia, Blackpool, Edinburgh, Dunfermline and is now in Singapore! She has been featured in various outlets in Asia using these two sources.

25 Facebook Lightbulb Entrepreneur & Press Hangout group

OK, so this one isn't free. But it's very cheap for what you get! And you can't afford to not be a part of it, if you want coverage.

Lightbulb is the only platform where you can pitch yourself directly (and in real-time) to thousands of journalists. The press members also post in the group all day long, looking for interviewees and guests for articles, TV and radio. This is the quickest way to snap up publicity. Members are in the national press every single day.

Because Lightbulb is hosted in a Facebook group, the discussions are live. So, when a TV producer posts and asks for a guest to appear on ITV's *This Morning*, you are able to respond and can get booked immediately. Lightbulb does not allow public relations people to join. This means the press can speak directly to their interviewees, without a go-between holding up deadlines.

But this is the one and only piece of spending money on PR that I would advise is worth paying for. At the point of publishing it is currently £5.99 (including VAT) per month. But it is so worth it for the real-time information provided. It's a rolling contract, so to try it out you just pay for an initial month then renew if you find it useful. You can cancel at any time.

Many thousands of entrepreneurs and journalists are in the group. Every single day there are numerous requests for experts and case studies. You can also pitch an idea for a journalist to pick up. Every week there is a very long list of successes. Many, many case studies you read or hear about in various news media come from this group!

If you do pitch an idea, remember to have an angle which will appeal to readers/viewers, not just "Here's my stuff, I want you to buy it"! Journalists may look for somebody who has a goat in the back garden or who has lost 100 kilos in weight, whatever! Remember, you don't have to be talking about your business to get PR coverage. They may be looking for someone who has been saved by a rhino whilst running away from a leopard. But much more likely are stories on relationships and topical issues.

It is a great place to keep an eye on regularly every day, as you never know what story you've got that might fit what a journalist is looking for and therefore get your business mentioned. And it gives you PR that you can put on your website. So, for example, if your business is or isn't related to the article, YOU are, so you can still say "As seen in…"

The group also contains guides for helping with your media involvement.

The group is run by Charlotte Crisp, a very experienced journalist, who is present daily and always cheerleading everyone.

A word of warning: There are other directories/groups/copycats you could join, even with 'free' elements. However, they come and go and it is not really worth paying to be listed in anything else. Lightbulb is the biggest, most established, best-known and most highly respected and you are unlikely to reach other people by joining copycat groups. Just about every media outlet is represented in Lightbulb.

26 Don't use "I've been on the telly, so pay me to join my database"

In a similar vein, be wary of anyone who is not in PR who says they can get you media coverage if you pay them a subscription. For example, I have seen someone claim that because they've been on the television they can get you on the television! This is just not true.

I've been in the media a lot. You can see the work it takes to get into the media from this book! There is no way somebody who is not a PR, who does not do PR for a living, can achieve this for someone else just by sending an email! If you are going to pay anyone make sure it's their core business. Only a couple of times in over 10 years have I had a journalist ask if I know of anyone who could help with an article.

That help would be related somehow to the work I do. So, for example, wanting another consumer champion to contact. That's where a relationship exists or I'm already in conversation with them.

There's no way I would be asked if I knew a doctor or a car mechanic to comment on that specialist field! Journalists use methods that reach a wider group, as detailed in this book.

27 FeatureMe! UK

FeatureMe! UK is a Facebook group run by two feature writers, Jill Foster and Sadie Nicholas, who work for the tabloids, with other journalists also posting. Journalists send requests for case studies, the majority of which are paid, too.

Dalia Hawley was in *Boots Health & Beauty* magazine in a feature for "I do Christmas my Way", she got paid £200 and the PR.

The two women who run it are lovely and I've done a few pieces with Jill Foster, for the *Daily Express* and *Daily Mail*.

Again, it doesn't have to be work-related. They might be looking for unusual experiences and are open to hearing about your ideas, too. Their focus is on lifestyle pieces about real people in their everyday lives.

They also take small contributions and will pay you. For example, I received £50 for talking about being a nanny.

Hundreds of FeatureMe! UK members appear in the press and it's a great way to either boost your profile, highlight a cause or simply have a bit of fun and earn a few pounds. They've done features covering subjects from new kitchen devices to innovative cancer treatments and everything in between.

28 Make The Headlines

You can submit your story idea to Make The Headlines. The team will assess whether they think they can pitch your story and, if successful, you will get paid for it.

They are also on Instagram where Linda Scerri saw a post seeking people with money saving ideas.

See **15** Check Instagram.

29 Focus on what you want to be known for

Work out your requirements and why you need the PR. Decide the field in which you want to be known as an expert. You need to be clear and focused. This will help you be intentional in what you do and to what you respond. Responding to all sorts of requests can confuse people. For example, I am known for being a consumer expert which means that I often get tagged in requests in groups like Lightbulb but also other networking groups. If people don't know what it is you stand for you won't get tagged and will miss opportunities.

Also, if you are constantly pitching and responding to requests in groups, then you will look desperate!

That isn't to say that you can't respond to something that isn't work-related or have opinions! But if you claim to have done every job under the sun, or had every type of relationship there is, then it won't do you any favours in the long term.

30 Don't antagonise journalists!

Regardless of what you may think about certain outlets or specific journalists, criticising them in public is not a good move! Recently in Lightbulb someone put a post about an article in the *Daily Mail*. She was providing an opinion, using the information from the article, and was offering comment. Somebody decided to have a go at her saying that it wasn't global news (it was in the *Daily Mail*, which has the largest circulation in the UK, alongside the *Telegraph*).

He suggested that journalists and members of the group were spreading misinformation. He was told by Charlotte, the group owner, to stop. I told him that journalist-bashing wasn't a very sensible idea when you want PR! Despite this, he continued and was rightly ignored and comments turned off. He then left the group and won't be getting PR from journalists any time soon.

31 Answer the question!

When you are in a group on Facebook in which journalists ask for case studies or examples, don't try and shoehorn yourself in!

It is OK to ask for clarity or if something fits, without pushing your luck, but to ask a journalist if they have "Thought about taking x angle?" or "I have done this" which doesn't fit the brief is both rude and extremely annoying for the journalist. The journalist is making a request for what they need. Whether you think they should take another angle or not is plain rude. In fact, you will occasionally also see people do this in the Lightbulb Facebook group.

The group rule "Please do not judge journalists' features; their commissions are not up for debate. Please DO comment under press requests if you'd like to take part or positively contribute" is robustly enforced. There will be a reason why journalists are asking what they asking, so it is important to respect it.

When looking for examples of tips for this book, I listed a few of the points. A couple of people tried to shoehorn in their press coverage. It's a waste of everyone's time. The reason I didn't ask for examples that they gave was because I already had those covered.

One even went so far as to say that they had got their coverage specifically in one of the ways on my list. I thought it was really good but, on conversing more, it absolutely wasn't true. She had got great coverage but not in the way I needed.

In another example, I asked for a short paragraph to explain how they had achieved the tip but instead got screenshots of the coverage. That didn't answer the question!

32 Sell your story

Some PR companies specialise in selling your story to a media outlet and then taking a cut of the payment. These may be useful for getting your news out there.

However, some outlets also provide an email address for "Got a Story?" For example, on *The Sun* and *Mirror* websites you will see "Got a story? Contact us with the details." They will write up the article and may pay you for your contributions to it. But again, make sure that you have a unique and interesting angle, as a journalist will not want to work with just a straight product/service pitch. Magazines such as *That's Life* will also pay for stories.

33 Give the journalist what they ask for in the way they asked for it!

This seems so obvious but it's amazing that some people expect journos to spend time looking for what they need from you and you could easily give.

Recently, a PR company emailed me asking if I wanted to interview their client, for *The Complaining Cow Consumer Show*.

I said yes.

I asked for a bio, headshot and all the links they'd like as I put it on my website.

I sent them a Zoom link.

They told me they would send me a Zoom link (after I sent one)

CHAPTER 1 Starting to get publicity in mainstream media

They sent me a link to the website.

I said please send me the bio and headshot and links as requested.

I got what was clearly a copy and paste from the website (didn't look but clearly was) no pic and no links.

I asked again for the pic and links.

I got a picture.

I asked again for the links.

Was asked "What links!"

I said social media, website and books etc?

Got sent her website again.

I asked him to confirm that there were no social media links.

He said all her links are on the website.

So I told him that it's really helpful to journos and saves them time if they're given what they request in the format they request!!

I then got a screen shot of her X (formerly Twitter) feed. It would have been quicker to send the link!

So I asked for the link.

Got it and an Instagram link.

At this point the show had run every week for a year. Every single person had sent what I asked for. (Other than one who told me to "Google me for more info!") The fact that this woman had engaged a PR company shows that if you are going to pay a company to do your PR work for you, then make sure they are doing what they are paid for and giving journalists what they request.

34 Treat a call from a journalist as an audition

When a journalist phones or emails to discuss the possibility of you being interviewed on a show or as a case study in the printed media, just be yourself. If you are being considered as a possible guest, don't worry if it's a news topic recently out that you haven't seen or heard about. That will be fine. If it's in your area of expertise, you'll be OK! Ask them to send you a link to the story. Don't be afraid to ask questions, not least if there is an appearance fee!

Jill Foster advises "Usually the journalist will want to do a phone or Zoom interview so set aside some time to talk to them in detail. Be prepared that they may need to call you back several times to check details."

She adds "Be the best interviewee you can be by making some notes of what you want to say to the journalists and thinking of specific anecdotes to illustrate your story. For instance, rather than say something like: 'I hated my job doing X' say something more like: 'I'd dread Monday mornings and could barely sleep with the worry of work the next day'…it really helps paint a picture of your story."

35 Don't ghost. Ever

This really annoys journalists!

A freelancer pitching a story about an individual, who then stops responding, is a sure-fire way to really rile a journalist. It's incredibly disrespectful. Whatever your reason for doing it, it's not acceptable. Even if you break the **36 Be sure you want to do it** rule, at least apologise. It's unprofessional and journalists do talk to each other.

Mel Fallowfield has been a freelance journalist for over 17 years for tabloids and women's magazines and has experience of people ghosting and finds it extremely frustrating. She comments:

"Like any self-employed person you rely on your reputation that you can deliver what you say you will on time. While you expect some people might have second thoughts—which is of course fine—what isn't OK is just to disappear, leaving me with a tight deadline and not knowing whether to move on or wait for them to get back to you. As a writer I spend a lot of time finding the perfect person for the article, be it the case history or an expert, and it is beyond frustrating for them to disappear. It shows a lack of courtesy and respect for deadlines and the work I do. And it would make me think twice about using them again as I simply don't have time to waste."

36 Be sure you want to do it

People changing their minds after the journalist has spent time pitching to their editor and writing the piece is annoying for journalists, similarly to ghosting. It happens far more than it should, is rude and disrespectful and, frankly, not fair on the journalist. It reflects badly on the journalist and if they are a freelancer you have potentially lost them money when you change your mind.

If you think someone you care about might not like what you are saying, ask them about it before agreeing to be a case study. Think about every angle of why you would or wouldn't want to be involved before, not after, the journalist has done the work getting the article agreed with their editor.

Similar to Mel Fallowfield and her frustrations with ghosting, Jill Foster warns "Don't agree to take part in the story and then back out. Journalists understand that life happens, that people get sick, die or have accidents. But if you've simply 'changed your mind', the press may consider you as 'unreliable'."

Even responding to requests and then changing your mind can be frustrating. For this book I got back to someone whom I chased and she said she "didn't mind" if I included her. So I didn't. Remember, you are getting PR and be respectful.

37 Don't always expect links

Hyperlinks, of course, are great. They help drive traffic to your site, but they are not and should not be the focus of your PR. Being out there, being seen, being heard and regularly is far more important than a hyperlink. If you are a blogger who relies on sponsored posts you will know that hyperlinks help your domain authority, but don't forget the PR value too.

If the hyperlink is really important to you, agree that there will be one before you give your information. Sometimes I'm told I will get a link. Sometimes they appear, sometimes they don't. Sometimes I get told I won't have a link and some of those times I decided not to spend my time putting together the information. It all depends on the piece and outlet in question.

Never blame the journalist or have a go at them! It will always be the editor's decision if the hyperlink goes in and a journalist will try their best if they have said they will do so.

Lizzie Cernik, a freelance journalist who writes mainly for *The Guardian*, says:

"Journalism isn't about giving people links to businesses, it's about publishing newsworthy, informative content. If you're an expert in a certain area then contributing to an article (even without a link) is good for your brand as your name will be in there and you can link back to it on your own website. It might be that people read it and want to find out more about you. There may also be other opportunities for future coverage where you do get a link."

38 Respond to feedback

If a journalist or producer responds to your pitch with feedback, please email them back and say "Thank you"! The lack of people's manners irritates me but I'm not alone. You never know when you may have another idea. If you were rude the first time they may well not look at you as favourably as they might have done.

East London Radio received a pitch from a vet who was very blatantly just wanting PR and not really offering anything. The station asks for donations from commercial organisations. The station editor suggested she might be able to get something to work and a donation to an animal charity might be good. She didn't reply which I believe is rude. Those of us who have ever had pets are well aware that if she had gained one customer it would very quickly have more than paid for a small donation!

39 Hashtag warning

Be careful of people and agencies offering services that aren't quite what they appear. For example, a PR company may put out a message with the hashtag *#JournoRequest*. However, they are not a journalist. So they are not looking for case studies, they are looking for journalists. It is the wrong hashtag to use but some do it!

Occasionally, a PR company/person may put out a hashtag and in fact it is looking for a company with which to do a story and charge for it. Some PR companies will be seeking comment to add to a project they are already doing, though. Just tread carefully and work with reputable people.

If you choose to pay someone who has the contacts to carry out some PR work for you, do your due diligence first. Research their previous work and probe existing clients by requesting references. Ask for recommendations in network groups.

40 Have photos ready and consider professional photos

You can take good photos on your phone, but make sure the lighting is clear and the resolution is high. Use the same one on all your social media to help brand consistency.

Consider professional photographs, especially when you have some PR under your belt. OK, so this will cost you money but it is worth it. Professional photographers have spent a lot of time honing their skills, will take better pictures than you and show you off in the best light, literally (unless you are a photographer of course!) Some outlets will send a photographer but if you have high resolution photos to offer, it can make you more appealing as a subject. It's not essential but worth thinking about when you start to get PR and you can use these photos as gifts, on social media etc., then think of the PR angle as free!

Make sure you have some landscape format photos too. These are often wanted by journalists and are frequently placed at the top of articles and used for social media. Ask the journalist what they need when sending them. Offer a variety when asked for photographs of you or your product. Think about what you might need for social media, too. Ensure you have some suitable square ones for Instagram posts, for example.

Take different outfits so you can have a mix of looks, such as professional and business-like and casual.

Jill Foster says "When it comes to photoshoots, you may need to travel or a photographer may come to you—ask upfront about it. If the journalist asks you for 'collects' this means pictures from your own collection that illustrate your story—so perhaps pictures of you when you were young or when you were pregnant/ill/winning the award etc."

41 Sending good photos

If you are asked to send photos and it's for print, make sure you send high resolution ones. Images should be at the best quality you can get otherwise the editor may not be able to use them.

Don't send photos via Facebook messenger because they will not be high resolution when downloaded.

42 Have your biography ready

This is useful to have because it means you can respond to journalists very quickly. I have various bios with different angles and different lengths to just copy and paste when needed.

For example, one includes the background about working in children's services, another that has the story of why and how I started the blog and yet another about how I developed the blog to work with businesses, etc.

43 Consider a media pack

Some people also have a media pack (also known as a press pack) which provides a biography, website and social media links, photos and previous media appearances. This can make it easy for the journalist to quickly see what you are about.

Punteha van Terheyden says that a media pack is really helpful, especially pictures. "In my own work, if I don't have pictures, I won't be sending a pitch out."

44 Try a cheeky request or stunt

Most, if not all, of the other examples in this chapter are conventional proven ways to work but sometimes a bit of creativity can work. Lisa Johnson, a business strategist, emailed the editor of *Psychologies* magazine and told her she thought they would get on and did she fancy a cocktail! She was concerned that this was a rookie error but she got a page spread, so it worked, no problem.

45 Media Matchmaker

Media Matchmaker is a media alert service. Journalists sign up to send out requests to individuals/brands that sign up.

You can sign up for free and sometimes there is a two week free trial. There is a lot of other useful stuff there as well. It is similar to **23 Response Source** above but has additional features, such as being able to join a searchable database and add videos if you use the paid for service.

Use this link *https://mediamatchmaker.co.uk/freecow/* for a free two week trial for readers of this book.

Jenetta Barry is the Founder of World Jenny's Day (10 October). She received significant coverage as a result of using Media Matchmaker during 2022. For example, a BBC Radio interview, a spot on *ITV News* during Suicide Prevention Week, *New!* magazine, *The Daily Mirror* and *OK! Magazine* online.

46 Talent Talks

This is an agency that casts extras for productions, such as music promos, TV & film, adverts and virals.

There is a subscription fee but you can also set up a free profile. Jobs on offer include being an extra in campaigns and film roles ranging from a few hours to a couple of days.

Again, this would be more to add to the media CV if you find work here. And it's paid work. Simply go to the Talent Talks website and sign up. You will have to pay to apply for any job. If you are successful in getting the role, you'll then be able to list it on your website as media work you have undertaken.

47 Unicorn Casting

You can sign up to Unicorn Casting to receive casting calls via WhatsApp. Also follow Unicorn Casting on Instagram which has regular flyers from production companies and agencies looking for presenters for branded content, people to take part in programmes, such as reality shows and quizzes.

48 Triangle News

Triangle News is an agency to which you can submit a story and it will help place it for you in a newspaper, magazine on the radio on TV and get you a fee. You can also send in pictures and videos and be paid for them.

49 Write a book

I wrote my first book *How to Complain: The Essential Consumer Guide to Getting Refunds, Redress and Results!* in 2014 because there was a gap in the market.

There is no doubt that writing a book gives you additional credibility in terms of public relations. If possible, ask someone respected in your sector to do a foreword and/or reviews. Paul Lewis and David McClelland reviewed that book, which gave it extra credibility.

By the time I wrote my second book, *101 Habits of an Effective Complainer*, I had worked many times with Paul, who wrote the foreword and review. I had also collaborated with Rob Rinder and Matt Allwright, so their reviews added credibility too.

Because a book gives you credibility, it means outlets are more likely to choose you when researching for guests. Your name is more likely to crop up in searches for subject experts. You can also give them as gifts to outlets. Left around the production offices, a book will keep you in the minds of team members for future appearances.

The Reedsy Blog provides links to numerous resources for getting started in writing a book.

50 Don't get concerned about 'vanity publishing'

Some people will say that self-publishing is vanity. I disagree. I know of people who are holding out for a traditional deal and that's vanity, when they could be waiting a long time. In that same time they could have the book out, helping them to raise credibility and awareness.

Lisa Johnson was given a book deal with an advance for *Make Money Online*. She still paid for a lot of her own marketing but has turned down a second book offer because she wants to be in control and make more money.

If you have no idea where to start, ask in Facebook network groups for recommendations of people who can help you to write and publish your book and go through the different routes to publishing. It's also helpful to get the idea out of your head and onto paper as soon as possible. Make sure you check anyone out thoroughly and see how many books they have helped with over how many years.

Listen to podcasts about people who write books and how they went about it.

Glean all the information you can along the way.

51 Get in someone else's book

There are a lot of people mentioned in this book and you will probably look up at least one. Even if it's just to check the type of media coverage or how it was written etc., the person in question is still getting more eyeballs on them and their business.

Paul Lewis in his book *Money Box: Your toolkit for balancing your budget, growing your bank balance and living a better financial life* recommends my book *How to Complain: The Essential Consumer Guide to Getting Refunds, Redress and Results!*

Caroline Bramwell is a PR and marketing mentor and features in Louise Minchin's book *Fearless: Adventures with Extraordinary Women*. Caroline met Louise a few years ago when their first autobiographies came out at the same time. Caroline tagged her in posts and she started following her. Then she approached her via Instagram. Louise then nominated Caroline to be one of her "Extraordinary Women", as she's been advocating for an active life with an ostomy—taking on Ironman challenges with a stoma, to break the taboo of "you can't do that" after stoma surgery.

She says "I've seen a distinct hike in my social media followers as a result".

See also **74** Network and **230** Start a Facebook group full of your ideal clients.

52 Collaborate on a book

Consider collaborating with others to publish a book. For some this hasn't led to any PR coverage but planned well, and with the right topic, it can work. Lisa Williams is a Vision Board Coach and collaborated with 15 female entrepreneurs on sharing their stories of how they stepped into their passion, purpose and power. Each story in their book *Seen* is a personal testament of inner strength and resilience. Although each woman's path has been unique, they share common elements of pain, loss, love and overcoming adversity to give them the courage to be the women they are today.

It was successful from a PR point of view because each author sent their own individual press release in their regions which allowed multiple opportunities for exposure. Lisa got coverage of her story about miscarriage in "Rhyl businesswoman shares story of miscarriages to inspire others 'in darkness'" in the *Rhyl Journal*.

Do your research before committing. In researching this book and looking for people who had been successful, there were several (who didn't want to be named for obvious reasons!) who said they wouldn't do it again, as it didn't lead to sales or PR. So, ask a lot of questions around what PR/marketing will be undertaken for the book, sales of similar books, the organiser, etc.

53 Keep up-to-date with current thinking

Keep your practice and knowledge up-to-date. This will help ensure that you are current when offering expertise, as well as help develop your business. Find the conferences, seminars, magazines, organisations and podcasts in your line of work.

Ellora Coupe is the founder of "Her Own Space", a women-only community about sustainability for interior design in UK homes. She attends a lot of conferences and expos, such as Futurebuild, and reads mainly online magazines, including *Passive House Plus*. Ellora finds podcasts like *Zero Ambitions* and *Air Quality Matters* very useful in her area of work.

54 Avoid a conflict of interest

This is really important. It is where you have competing interests. If you are likely to receive personal benefit from doing something without declaring it, that would be a conflict of interest. Sometimes even declaring it would not be enough. For example, I do not take payment for endorsing products. As a consumer champion I have to remain independent and people would not trust me to give an independent opinion on a company if it were also paying me to say nice things. It would be the same principle for sponsored posts. Even if I declared them, it would diminish trust in me for some people.

This is deeply frustrating because companies have offered to pay me a lot for sponsored posts, reviews and links to their sites! I've said "no" to a lot of opportunities! But would you trust someone to be independent if they were also paid to publish something, even if they declared it?

So, ask yourself before any paid exposure, what would your customers think? Would they trust your advice if you are an expert on pets and you were paid to host an advert on your website, even if you declared it?

It's not just about being paid either. Other conflicts of interest might be having to discuss a competitor or a product sold by one or going against your own values.

Janine McDonald turned down the opportunity to be on TV when the producers wanted her to declutter the whole house of one of her clients who has autism, ADHD, hoarding tendencies and other medical issues. As her client preferred to work in hour and a half blocks, she turned down the opportunity, wanting to do what was best for her client, not the production company.

See **276** Don't be afraid to say "no".

55 Could a customer have a story?

Look at your customers. Have any of them got an interesting story or journey with which your product or service has helped? Have you got a case study you could use? You might be able to work together on getting joint PR by using one of the methods in this book.

Nicola Toner, a crowdfunding mentor, worked with one of her clients on a pitch and approached the *Derby Telegraph* when her client's crowdfunding campaign launched. Dan Smith was raising funds to complete the purchase of his local pub The Red Lion, where he had been landlord for nearly ten years. He was short of £50,000 and was crowdfunding to prevent it being sold to someone else. The piece ran online as "Landlord needs £50k more to save village pub from being sold off" and in the printed paper in October 2022. The paper then did a follow up piece, "Meet Red Lion licensee who has bought his pub after 10 years" when the purchase was completed in March 2023.

56 Use Medium to publish articles

Medium is a publishing platform where professional and amateur authors can share their writing on any topic. Writers are from around the world, with a majority of American contributors.

You could use this to practise writing and promoting yourself on social media and see what is popular. Remember, just as with posting anywhere else, it is not for advertising your products or services, it is about giving value to the readers and boosting your profile as the expert.

There is an option to pay a membership fee of five dollars a month which gives you access to some more content and the option to be paid for your work. This is based on how long people spend reading your content and how many 'claps' it gets (similar to 'likes' on Facebook).

CHAPTER 1 Starting to get publicity in mainstream media

57 Pitch to *Authority Magazine*

Medium hosts *Authority Magazine* which publishes in-depth interviews with notable figures in business, culture and other fields. It lists the subjects of articles it is working on and invites potential interviewees on this page:

At the point of publishing, the list was around 400 across multiple subject areas. So, you have a good chance of being featured.

58 Work with PR companies

A PR company may approach you for input. So, instead of paying a PR company work with one! They might ask you for comment or to collaborate on an article with them. They may offer you payment for this too.

For example, a PR company contacted me for comment on a report that they had written for a client. Although they offered a fee, I did it for free because I have to remain independent, but it would still be PR for me.

See **54 Avoid a conflict of interest**. The PR company sent out a press release and so did I. *Good Housekeeping* used the information from the press release (in which I was quoted) and contacted me for further comments.

59 Use your vulnerabilities

The press love stories of adversity, tragedy, challenge and controversy. You'll see them in the women's magazines all the time. Be sure that you are at peace with any story and that you are happy to share it.

See **36 Be sure you want to do it**, **154 Ignore the trolls on online articles**, **155 Ignore the trolls on social media too** and **156 Be prepared to not be fully happy!**

Maddy Alexander-Grout, founder of Mad About Money, says "I make myself vulnerable to criticism all the time! In fact only today someone totally came at me and accused me for being 'woe is me' because I talked about my business failing and my ADHD. I always show up as me. I tell the truth, good or bad. If you tell the truth you can't get caught out."

The article "My spending addiction left me £40k in debt", published on *Yahoo UK News*, covers Maddy's story in which she talks about depression, being in debt and the relationship with her mother.

Dr Marianne Trent, Clinical Psychologist, author and Host of *The Aspiring Psychologist Podcast*, says:

"Being brave and doing something a bit different can feel a bit exposing and vulnerable inducing. It can be useful when considering PR options whether you'd be comfortable with strangers knowing this information about you. It's ideal if you can be in a position where you are making mindful choices which keep you within your zone of tolerance.

However, sometimes people may have strong opinions on us and our work and may misinterpret something which has evoked a strong reaction in them. This means they might well want to take action to control or process the way they feel by connecting and discussing it with others in a public forum.

Some pretty solid advice to bear in mind is that 'good stuff rarely happens in the comments!' The majority of people are likely to read or watch your work and then take no further action. People who take to the keyboards and phones to get involved with after event commentary might well not be an honest representation of the majority of public opinion and it's fair to say they're also unlikely to be your ideal client."

60 Be controversial in mainstream media

Samantha Jayne is a Spiritual Coach, helping women in the areas of money, success, self-love, dating and valuing themselves.

She wrote "Why I'll never date a man who is paid less than me" for the *Daily Mail*, together with journalist Samantha Brick. It's a piece that was guaranteed to get huge engagement and many comments below the line.

The article was then sold to an online magazine in Switzerland and to *The Sun*. She was further asked to appear on the *Jeremy Vine* show, as well as on *BBC Wiltshire* and *BBC Gloucester* radio.

CHAPTER 1 Starting to get publicity in mainstream media

If you do something like this then see **36** **Be sure you want to do it**, **154** **Ignore the trolls on online articles**, **155** **Ignore the trolls on social media too** and **156** **Be prepared to not be fully happy!**

See also **130** **Be controversial on air** and **239** **Be controversial on social media**.

61 Consider your brand

Think carefully about what you want covered in the media. For example, one person in Lightbulb worked with children. He also had a band. He pitched about a "rude" comment from a woman who told him to put his genitalia away when he performed whilst wearing an outfit that was very loose. He wanted a journalist to write about this as "body shaming".

A number of journalists asked him whether he really wanted "willy" references associated with his name when people googled him? Particularly when this sort of article would get a huge number of comments below the line. And he was adamant that he should be allowed to talk about it. Of course, anyone should be able to discuss whatever they want. However, brand image is important.

62 Listen to the experts!

Take **61** **Consider your brand** as an example. This advice came from a number of very experienced journalists and people in business. It would be sensible to listen to advice from these people. It's free consultancy! And, if you are wanting free PR, who better to tell you the pros, cons and what will happen with the resulting PR than journalists?

63 Get reviews from customers

This is really important as it adds to your credibility. Currently, there's a lot of doubt about whether online reviews are genuine. So, where possible, ask for video reviews, simply get out your phone and ask someone to briefly talk about your product or service when you see them. They can only say "no"! Also, if appropriate, put the person's job title and link to their website so that people can check it out.

Most people just don't think to do this, but it isn't hard! For example, Lindsay Edwards, a personal stylist, wondered how she could get reviews. I suggested that every time she works with a client and they say something like "I never would have chosen that outfit, but it looks great, thank you" that she just gets out her phone and ask them to say it onto the recording! So simple but effective and she is now doing this, adding lots of value and credibility to her brand.

If you don't see the customer in person, use a free platform like VideoAsk. You simply send them a link and they can record something and send it back.

Journalists are likely to check out your website and social media as part of their due diligence.

When asking for a review, give the customers an outline of what you would like them to include. This could be in the form of a checklist which will help them and give you what you need, including quantified detail of how you helped them get from A to B. Thanks to dynamic copywriter and coach, Georgina L Nestor, for these pointers:

"A quantified testimonial goes beyond the usual 'I bought this and it was great' comment by providing concrete, measurable results that help potential clients or customers gauge the efficacy of a product or service.

It offers credibility and specificity, making the testimonial more compelling and trustworthy. For instance, stating 'This service helped boost my sales by 30%' is far more impactful and persuasive than a generic statement of satisfaction. It illustrates a direct correlation between the service used and the improvement seen, offering a clearer picture of potential benefits.

Moreover, quantified testimonials allow for a more accurate comparison between different products or services, thus aiding in the decision-making process. Ultimately, they provide an authentic, tangible measure of value that generic praise cannot achieve.

When you're asking for a testimonial from a client or customer, send them the following guidelines. These points will result in a much more effective testimonial as readers will understand the depth of their experience better and how your product or service was instrumental in effecting their transformation."

Georgina offers these tips on what to send to your clients when requesting

CHAPTER 1 Starting to get publicity in mainstream media

a testimonial:

"1. Begin by describing the issue you were facing. Let's say you were struggling to get your online business off the ground or you weren't making enough sales—explain that.

2. Proceed to discuss why you chose our product or service. Did a friend rave about us, or maybe one of our email newsletters caught your eye?

3. Now, tell us how we made a difference. For instance, did our strategies help you tackle that online business issue head-on? Walk us through the journey, from where you started (say, no idea about marketing) to where you ended up (like, booming business!).

4. Now, it's crucial to highlight the concrete results. Did your sales go up by 20%? Or perhaps you're raking in an extra £500 each month? The more specific, the better!

5. Lastly, let's chat about if you'd put in a good word for us. Would you recommend us to your fellow online entrepreneurs? Or perhaps to anyone trying to make a dent in the digital world?"

And there you go! That's a perfect recipe for a super-useful testimonial that'll take pride of place on your website, social posts, or in your email marketing efforts.

64 Get reviews from people in the media

You can even ask people in the media industry if they will give you a review. If you have built up a good relationship with them you could connect on LinkedIn. (A note here though that this sector as a whole is not very active on there). You could request a testimonial and then take this and put it on your website.

For example, I worked with Jill Foster a couple of times, contributing to an article for *The Guardian* and one for the *Express* and asked her to write me a testimonial on LinkedIn. She said:

"I've worked with Helen on features for national newspapers and there's no one better when it comes to getting quotes on how to complain effectively. Her consumer knowledge is second to none. She is forensic when it comes to detail and will gladly provide extra information at a moment's notice—invaluable to busy journalist with tight deadlines. I'd have no hesitation at all in recommending her to any other media professional."

I wouldn't recommend this for short appearances but if you've been with them all day and built up a good rapport, ask them to do you a quick testimonial on your phone. Make a joke about being the other side of the camera!

This can help show your personality, too. For example, when I worked with Steve Blears, a producer/director on *Rip Off Britain*, we had a good laugh and his testimonial on LinkedIn showed that, too:

"Slayer of poor customer service, tireless advocate of the downtrodden consumer, supporter of businesses who respect their clientele. Chocolate fan. TV presenter. All round good egg and occasional pain in the arse."

If you don't ask, you don't get! You will see on my website that I have many testimonials from journalists, TV, directors, producers, and well-known presenters.

65 Keep things simple

If you're investigating an area of work, perhaps something that has piqued your interest, then if you are thinking in PR terms, make sure it is a simple subject!

Although not undertaken for PR purposes, a colleague and I investigated the inadequate approval and monitoring of Alternative Dispute Resolution (ADR) providers. It would have been a time-consuming topic to delve into for PR purposes.

Whilst the body of work and the continuing of work on reporting on ADR is recognised by those who understand it, we have been told numerous times by journalists, that it is too complicated to report on! The reports are listed with other academic research into ADR, have been referenced a couple of times in two broadsheets, a professor's university report and Which? but that's the limit over the years.

So, if you wish to investigate a topic in-depth, first research your market and your potential audience to determine whether it is worth the time and energy.

66 Send gifts

If you make something a little out of the ordinary, send a producer an example! Everyone loves a present. Only a rude person (and there are too many around!) would not at least contact you to say thank you. This helps build a relationship. My milk sweets in old-school milk bottles went down well! Now I send books that I know the recipients will use!

Unusual/lovely/useful products are likely to stay around in the office and keep your name out there.

Julie Čolan, founder of Secret Whispers, which sells pelvic floor products and raises pelvic floor issues awareness, wanted her Kegal Weights Kit to be mentioned on the *Chris Evans Radio Show* on Virgin Radio. After presenter Rachel Horne appeared on the show discussing her pelvic floor issues, Julie found a PR email address for the show and asked if she could send her a kit. She replied, providing her address. To ensure that the kit was not just thrown in the store room along with other freebies they must receive, she paid a woman to beautifully gift wrap three of her Kegal Kits, including printouts of all the free downloads. She then used a courier to deliver them individually to Rachel Horne, Chris Evans' wife Natasha and to the PR lady.

A month later she woke up to record sales, with her phone and laptop going crazy. Rachel Horne had said live on radio that she had her first "dry run" and was using Secret Whispers.

67 Work on your SEO

SEO is Search Engine Optimisation, the science (and art) of getting your website into search results on Google, Bing and Yahoo.

Keep on top of SEO on your website. A lot of outlets will search the web for an expert. I have been contacted many times from people searching for a complaints expert in XYZ subject. There are masses of free resources out there to help with your SEO. Sites like Semrush, SheerSEO, Wincher all have basic free packages which allow you to check your back links, competitors, keywords, etc. You can also use Google Analytics.

Even though I have been on many outlets a number of times and should already be on "source" databases, I still get enquiries through my website from researchers at outlets who have found me via an Internet search.

68 Apply for a reality show!

Okay, so I've never done this, nor would I! But let's be honest here, many people have gone on to have careers in the media from being on a reality show. However, this should not be your primary aim as it will just come across that you're not being the 'real you'. Make sure this is something that you will enjoy and can deal with the inevitable trolling, only for you to be forgotten five minutes later!

69 Keep an eye on messages

Check your email spam and the message requests which are often hidden on Facebook! If you are using Facebook or X (formerly Twitter) to respond to requests it is likely that journalists may respond by sending you direct messages, rather than responding on threads, to save time. People have been known to miss these messages and lose out on opportunities!

70 Giving your time and advice for no reward

When you have established yourself as an expert, producers and production companies will come to you for input. You'll find yourself giving lots of information in the belief that you will be used. Sometimes this is the case but other times it isn't.

For example, I have been contacted for thoughts on stories that have then not gone ahead. Often the work will go to someone better known and/or a presenter, rather than an expert. This can again be frustrating but I have learnt that this is quite normal in all areas of expertise.

A colleague with more knowledge and experience than me spent a long time

CHAPTER 1 Starting to get publicity in mainstream media

giving a production company lots of information for a television series, under the belief that he would at least contribute. The presenters had no knowledge or experience in the consumer arena and he eventually didn't appear in front of the camera. We both bemoaned this fact and debated whether we should charge for expertise, with the risk that they will just go somewhere else! Although difficult, we had to regard it as just a part of the learning experience!

Producers and commissioners will want a certain look to the programme they are making and often at the point of talking to you won't know who will be delivering the piece.

71 Don't worry if you have nothing to sell

When I started my blog, I had nothing to sell. In fact, it was a couple of years before I even published my first book. The blog was a hobby. But you can establish yourself as an expert right from the start. Within six months of starting my blog, I was asked by *BBC Radio 5* to do a phone in and I got paid for it. I also did *BBC Breakfast* (I didn't know at that point I could get paid for that one!) before doing those two major outlets, I had only written one small article for the local free paper!

72 Read the room

Be aware and sensitive to other people and what's going on in the world when you pitch. For example, someone in Lightbulb pitched a story about not being able to find a luxury watch on Bond Street. Few people want to hear about your excessive spending habits during a cost of living crisis when people can't afford to feed themselves and their children. Not only are you likely to offend people in the group, if you were to have a story like that picked up in the current financial climate (at the point of publishing), you would be unmercifully trolled.

See also **62 Listen to the experts**.

73 Accept that sometimes it's just not your turn!

The more media you do, the more you will find this. You get asked if you would be interested in covering a topic on the radio or TV and you get told you aren't needed but you see someone else cover the same item. Frustrating and disappointing as this may be, it doesn't mean you did anything wrong or they won't use you in the future. It's just that frequently the production team are looking at more than one person or they want a different dynamic between people.

74 Network

It pays to network everywhere. Don't be afraid to talk about your work, as you'll be surprised who knows whom. Kerry Hales (Kerry Hales Coaching) chatted to another mother one day on the train. The other mother worked at Sky TV and used to work at *BBC Radio 5*. She knew someone at *BBC Radio 5* and got Kerry an interview. Her book *Life Lessons from Your Knicker Drawer* returned to the best-seller list as a result.

75 Ask the journalist where they heard about you

If you get contacted out of the blue for a comment or appearance, it's worth asking where they heard about you. This can help you see if your SEO is working, or what social media posts have been spotted, for example.

When the consumer editor of *That's Life* contacted me for an interview on complaining effectively, I asked how she had heard of me. She said it was from reading Paul Lewis' book that had mentioned my own book.

See **51** Get in someone else's work.

76 Honour exclusivity!

If you have agreed an exclusive contract with a journalist or outlet then you must stick to it. It would demonstrate a lack of integrity and professionalism to breach any contract. Furthermore, word will get round and you may face penalties.

77 Offer to write the article for the editor!

Do not do this to a journalist! But if you have written a number of articles over a few years and an editor contacts you and wants to pay you as a case study with all your expertise, you could offer to write the article for them.

For example, when the consumer editor of *That's Life* asked if I would be available for a half-hour interview to do a "How to Complain" article, I offered to write it for her for the same fee! I knew readers would get the most helpful information and it's easy for me to do. It wouldn't take much longer than the interview. In addition, she offered to include the name of my business and my books, with images, in the article.

Remember, at this point I had been a journalist for a few years and written two books, so she knew I had the credibility and ability to do the article. See **75 Ask the journalist where they heard about you** and you could do this without expecting to be paid if you are starting out. See also **19 Look at frequency**.

This also led to further work for me with *That's Life*. Note that it is getting more difficult to do this. I wrote a number of articles for the "money" series until the section was taken in-house.

78 Recommend other experts

When you've done media regularly for a few years and have built your relationships with other experts, do recommend them if you are not available to appear. For example, after I started to give quotes for Jasmine Birtles' work and she was interviewed on *The Complaining Cow Consumer Show* episode "Jasmine

Birtles explains interest, inflation & stagnation", we built a good working relationship, she started to recommend me to outlets and I reciprocated.

When outlets return to you because they trust you, they will also have confidence in your recommendations of other experts.

79 Adapt your approaches

Each journalists is unique! So, one type of approach may not work with another. When you start to get PR, accept any feedback and use appropriately, ensuring that it might not always be the case for everyone. For example, generally one follow-up after a pitch is acceptable but if you send a third some journalists would be really annoyed.

Some outlets prefer for you to pitch to a specific journalist, others to the outlet or media group. There will never be "one size fits all" and you should build a profile for each journalist and outlet you encounter, so you know the best ways to approach them.

80 Work on non-mainstream outlets too

When you plan for time to spend on PR, it's important to give a relevant weighting to non-mainstream media. They complement each other.

Non-mainstream media includes podcasts, social media and blogs. These outlets have the potential to reach as many people, sometimes more, so when you plan your PR consider the potential reach of everything.

See **CHAPTER 8 Boost your profile outside of traditional media**.

81 Pitching and press releases

Be proactive as well as reactive in trying to obtain PR. This means taking action to put yourself out there as well as responding to calls for case studies.

CHAPTER 1 Starting to get publicity in mainstream media

See **CHAPTER 6 Building your media contact list** and **CHAPTER 7 Sending out press releases**. As part and parcel of pitching to journalists in this chapter these two chapters complement this one as they help with putting ideas together and building contacts and relationships.

82 Get your images used

If you have lots of product images, try using Press Loft. PR companies and brands sign up and upload images for journalists to search. At the point of publishing there is a 60-day free trial. After this time you can pay per image or monthly.

When a journalist downloads an image from Press Loft you get a notification with the details of the publication and the journalist's name and email address.

Susan Bonnar, the founder of The British Craft House (TBCH), puts lots of her images on Press Loft. She has secured coverage in more than 20 outlets, including *Fabulous* magazine, *Chat* magazine Christmas gift guide, women's and crafts magazines. Susan says:

"I think we are super lucky to get so much coverage! On Press Loft when they download an image I follow it up with a thank you to the journalist and a short bio about the seller and TBCH! I think that helps in us getting journalists who regularly use us!"

See also **148 Thank journalists appropriately**.

83 Set up news alerts for your name

Google Alerts can be configured so that whenever a word (or words) appears online, you will get an email alert.

The site will ask for your email address and the word(s) you want to be alerted about when they are mentioned on an Internet news channel. You will then be notified when those words appear.

Similarly, you can use TalkWalker. It's a good idea to use both, as they can miss stories. TalkWalker will pick up mentions in blogs and social media as well as news. Use " " around search phrases.

This is particularly useful if a journalist cannot tell you when the piece mentioning you goes live. It also means that if another outlet has picked up the story, you will get notified of that. For example, I get Google Alert notifications when another newspaper in the same media group uses a quote from an article to which I've contributed. DMG, for example, has a number of newspapers in the group and may use a quote you give in both the *Daily Mail* and *Metro*. But many outlets cite the *BBC News* website, so it can be covered across groups, too. I've also been notified when an outlet in New Zealand used a quote of mine from an article originally written for a UK newspaper!

When you get this alert, it's another outlet that you can add to the "as seen in" list and push out on social media. Your "as seen in" list and/or graphics demonstrates your credibility, showing that the media comes to you.

84 Help people out

If you are an expert in your field, you'll often get tagged in posts on social media as someone who could help. This happens to me frequently! I do offer help for free and usually signpost people to find the information on my blog. But occasionally a story might really catch on my interest, usually because it's a company that has behaved appallingly.

For example, I was tagged on a Facebook post written by Claire-Marie Kelly, a vulnerable customer of Utility Warehouse, who had been left without energy and it annoyed me intensely. So, I helped her with her issue. It then turned out that there was enough to make it a good story: "Mum who was switched to prepay energy meter without being told wins £620 in compensation" for the *Mirror*.

Usually, when you help people, it's just to be kind! But as you do it more, you may find that it will turn into a story if you can share it with a journalist, send out a press release or write up the article yourself.

85 Give great customer service!

You may wonder what this has to do with PR. But it's really essential. It is still about credibility and increases your reviews and referrals and therefore your presence.

CHAPTER 1 Starting to get publicity in mainstream media

There are numerous ways you can exceed customers' expectations, handle complaints well, provide a great customer journey from beginning to end and more. You can get lots of ideas from the business side of my website. You can also join my free Facebook group "Increase sales through customer service with care, compassion & integrity". This group is for discussion of all things customer service, including much useful advice from other small business owners.

You can also download my free resource "5 ways to get rave reviews and referrals".

86 Use Awareness Days/Weeks/Months to highlight your expertise

AwarenessDays.com provides many of these. You can send out press releases, respond to pitches and approach journalists direct. You may find that you don't get the coverage there and then but possibly later down the line.

Stacey Brown, founder of Lucky Penny Creations, released her book *Hear us Roar: 12 Women's Journeys with Endometriosis*, raising awareness, supporting women for Endometriosis Awareness month in March 2023 and was featured in *Chat* magazine in June of the same year.

87 Hold an event

If applicable to your business and you have a good following and contacts, hold an event. It could be a product launch or working with a charity, for example. You can then send a press release about the launch or write up an article after the event. Include some good quotes and videos from participants. There's nothing wrong with inviting a few celebrities or contacting some PR companies to ask if they know of anyone who might like to attend.

Having 'goodie bags' to take away is always a good move, too!

See **8 Invite the press to events**.

88 Have quotes ready

In order to be able to respond quickly to journalist requests, set up a spreadsheet or Word document with links to social media posts you have written that would make good quotes. Or, if you have a blog, simply search your blog for quotes. They are your own words and so there is nothing wrong with copying, pasting and tweaking and sending to journalists.

I send excerpts from my blog to journalists as quotes. They are my words and doing this saves me time!

89 Shout about your clients!

Share the success of a client. If you share your client's story and how you helped them, it's media coverage for both of you. They get media coverage, you get potential clients seeing first-hand how you can help them!

See also **22** **Undertake research with your ideal client and actual clients** and **54** **Avoid a conflict of interest**.

90 Think of a journey

Media outlets love a journey. People getting out of debt are always popular with the tabloids. For example, I wrote "Single mum's lockdown business coaching people on LinkedIn lets her ditch renting to buy her first home" for the *Metro*. See **21** **Research journalists and think about whether to typecast them**. This was an excellent piece of PR for Lea and resulted in a lot of sales for her.

91 Reply to journalists promptly

Journalists are often on tight deadlines, so even if you think you have given them the information they have asked for, if they come back asking for clarity on something then make sure you respond in a timely manner. I struggled to get the information from one person and in the end she missed the opportunity to be in the *Guardian* with a link to her product.

Punteha van Terheyden says "The best case studies are honest, exclusive, have a strong narrative, are happy to be pictured, easy to work with and have good recall."

CHAPTER 2

Prepare for your coverage

It is normal to get excited or worried and to doubt yourself but work through it!

My blog had been going for less than six months when I got my first media request, an email asking me to appear on a phone-in on *BBC Radio 5* late at night, for *The Phil Williams Show*. I was overwhelmed. Although I thought one man and his dog might be listening at the time, it was *BBC Radio 5* and it was live! And it was paid! Luckily I happened to be seeing my friend Sue that day for lunch. She calmed me down and reassured me that I could do it! Another old boss said simply "Talk slowly". This is great advice, although I'm not sure I always follow it but I remember it stuck with me for that first appearance! Why? Talking slowly helps to keep you calm.

---

92 Decide on your title

Decide how you would prefer to be described/introduced in your interview or quote. It won't always go in as you would like. Even after years of saying "Consumer Champion" I recently sent a press release with a comment and was still described in a national newspaper as being from a "Complaints Firm"! Be consistent with your brand, too, so that studio staff will describe you as you want to be known. Your name and title will be displayed as an 'Aston' or 'name strap' across the lower section of the TV screen.

93 Call yourself an expert!

I used to hate this! When asked if I wanted to be described as a consumer expert, I always said "no". It always sounded like a touch of arrogance! But, as I added more strings to my bow and became a consumer champion, author, journalist, blogger, speaker and business consultant, it became more difficult to know what title to use.

I want both consumers and businesses to look me up, as I help both. And really "consumer expert" was the only phrase that covered it, and I became more comfortable using that.

There is a commonly held belief that an expert is someone who knows more about a subject than everyone else in an average room. I think this is true and has helped a lot of people come to terms with using the word "expert".

94 Key points

Time goes VERY QUICKLY! Much more quickly than you think and sometimes the interviewer will talk for longer than is helpful. So, think about which points you most want to get across but be very careful not to over prepare or you may appear stilted.

95 Get everything in writing!

When you are booked, ensure that everything is in writing. For a television appearance, most often you'll get a phone call, so be sure to follow up in writing. Get everything about payment clarified. Travel and, if appropriate, accommodation, is usually arranged and paid for beforehand. Discuss and agree any payments for expenses, etc. If anything gets cancelled, you won't be out of pocket.

96 Practice on Zoom

If you're nervous, start a Zoom call with just you and record yourself. You can watch it back to check the lighting, how your outfit looks and decide if you want to change anything. Don't be too critical, you will be your harshest critic.

97 Back up plans!

Give your contact more than one telephone number and be ready to use your mobile phone hotspot if your main home/office wi-fi fails. Even consider having back up clothes in case you spill something! It is unlikely that things will go wrong but having back up plans will calm any nerves, increase your confidence and make your performance all the better.

98 Announce on social media

If you will be appearing on radio or television, announce on social media the name, date, time and channel of the programme. Retweet/share anything if you have been mentioned in a post.

Keep **112 Don't worry about cancellations!** in mind. I've never heard anyone say to me "I thought you were going to be on…" And, if they do, it is easily answered, without losing face!

99 Share your preparation

You want your audience to tune into your performance, as well as getting the message out that you are in the media. So tell them! If you are preparing something, talk about it or say that you are looking forward to talking to "x" and "y" at "z" time. Keep an eye out on X (formerly Twitter) for mentions of you, too, as often outlets say what guests they have coming on and will tag you and you should like and share those posts!

Build some mystery and take shots of the studio for a great reveal.

On social media, say that you are looking forward to being on the show at a given time, so viewers/listeners can see you will be in the media. But be aware that plans change and you could be dropped at any time! See **112 Don't worry about cancellations!**

100 Do a quick live or record a quick video

If you are able and it is possible (i.e. you won't be disturbing anyone), do a quick live on Facebook or a reel for Instagram. Video often gets more engagement than a still photo and if you also send a picture later you'll be using various formats at different times, reaching different audiences. Talk about what you are going to be covering, as this helps show off your knowledge and expertise, too!

101 Prepare appropriately

For most television and radio appearances you will have a conversation with the producer or presenter prior to the interview. You should expect to be thrown curveballs! It is highly likely that a producer or researcher may tell you about questions that you will be asked and the interviewer/presenter(s) won't ask them! Don't worry about it, that's normal. If you know your stuff, it won't be a problem!

Some outlets are much better than others at preparing guests.

Paul Lewis at *MoneyBox* on *BBC Radio 4* is the ultimate professional here. He takes a lot of time preparing with guests how the programme will go, the questions he would like to ask and discusses your answers, so that you are happy. The result is you go in thoroughly confident about how the programme will run and give a good performance, so it is a very sensible approach!

Make some notes and practice, so that you can safely go off-piste and still be natural.

If you are on the radio, take a few notes in the lead up to your segment. You can use them as nudges/reference points and even read from them if it answers a specific question and you can make it sound natural!

See **94 Key points** and **108 But don't over prepare!**

CHAPTER 2 Prepare for your coverage

102 Be rested

If you have enough warning, get to bed early and save the alcohol to celebrate afterwards! You want to look and sound your best!

103 Think about what clothes you will wear!

If you wear a dress, that microphone cable has to go up your dress to your neckline and the microphone clip fixed somewhere!

Wear something in which you are comfortable and which fits well. It doesn't matter how fantastic you look in a top if you are constantly readjusting it. Lindsay Edwards, a personal stylist, advises:

"If you plan to wear a new outfit for the first time, have a trial run first by sitting down in it at home, ideally in front of a mirror. You might notice that the outfit stretches or gapes in unexpected ways the moment you become seated. You don't want to make that potentially embarrassing discovery whilst on TV!"

Lindsay adds this tip, about necklines "High necklines, such as turtlenecks, can look great in reality. But on screen, the proportions can become lost, creating the illusion that your head is floating in mid-air!"

Finally, she recommends not to wear any clothing which constricts, pinches or feels itchy, no matter how fabulous you might look in it. "You simply cannot focus or express yourself with confidence if you're feeling uncomfortable. Take the time to find an outfit which you look and feel great in, you won't regret it."

If you want to really be safe, take a clothes brush with you to remove any hair you pick up, etc!

104 Think of colours you will wear

Think about the environment. For example, if you are going to be on the red sofa for *BBC Breakfast*, don't wear red!

Don't wear prints with close lines or spots, as these can sometimes cause a shimmering effect on screen. That includes ties. Annoyingly, a herringbone pattern is a 'no-no', too.

Avoid wearing black or white. The television cameras set their lighting range on the brightest and darkest objects in the room, so your face may be underlit or overlit but if you get good make-up you'll probably be OK!

105 Think about jewellery

A necklace is a great way to add interest to your portrait area, just ensure you get the length right. Lindsay says that the ideal necklace length to wear is 16-20 inches.

"Any longer and it will draw the audience's eyes downwards and is likely to be partially cut out of the frame."

However, think about how close the necklace is to the top of your outfit. The microphone is going to go here for TV and it may knock. Also, allow for any jewellery moving around! I am still learning this and if you ever see me without a necklace it's because the sound person made me take it off!

Big dangly earrings can be an off-putting distraction for viewers.

When in a radio studio, if you talk with your hands, beware clanking bracelets that will bang on the surface! Yes, I learnt that by that experience so you don't have to!

106 Think about make-up

For most live appearances, such as *BBC Breakfast*, you get hair and make-up done. Frankly, sometimes it feels like the best part, particularly if you are going out afterwards! But if it's not live you won't be getting hair and make-up done.

Some outlets will say they do top ups, such as *GB News*, but actually you might have two minutes! You want to ensure that you take any shine off your face with foundation or powder and if you have a bald head don't forget the top of your head, too!

107 Be ready to go if at work

If you don't work from home and you start to get live TV requests for topical issues that day, you might want to consider always wearing something you would be happy to be on TV wearing or have an outfit at work. The same applies for make-up and accessories.

108 But don't over prepare!

If you keep on practising everything and trying to be perfect you will tie yourself in knots. Jenny Leggott is the founder of Sammy Rambles, inventor of Dragonball and the author of numerous books.

She says:

"The first appearances I probably over-prepared, spending hours on hair, make-up, what to say, practice in the mirror, now I'm more relaxed and what you see is what you get. One habit I haven't broken is disappearing into the toilets for a minute beforehand just to get some quiet space to say to myself I can do this. The habit dates back to when I played volleyball and instead of finishing the physical warm up I'd go away for a minute to mentally prepare for the match. And we won lots of games!"

109 Trust in your abilities

Remember that you know your stuff or you wouldn't have been asked to do it. You can practice but don't overdo it or you won't come across naturally.

Before any appearance, especially if you're live, at a speaking event and new to publicity, give yourself a good talking to!

See **108** **But don't over prepare!**

110 Watch/listen to the programme before your appearance

This will you give a flavour of the style of the programme. It will also give you an idea of the types of questions the presenters ask.

111 Think positively!

Personally, I don't get too much into "positive thinking" as a day-to-day concept. But I do recommend concentrating on positive thoughts about going on the radio/TV.

Don't think about all the things that can go wrong, as if you focus on what can go wrong, it possibly will! My worst fear about live TV or radio is that I will swear! So, I focus on the things I will say, rather than what I will not say! If it's your bag, there are lots of free Facebook groups out there for positive thinking and manifesting positivity.

112 Don't worry about cancellations!

I have lost count of the times I have been booked for appearances and the broadcaster then cancelled on the day. Once I was even in the cab going to *BBC News* when they rang and told me to turn round! Don't let it knock your confidence, it's not about you. These last-minute changes happen because of constantly-fluctuating news priorities.

I was recently filmed for a *Channel 5 News* segment. It wasn't used, but I still did the work, so I invoiced. If a fee has been agreed then this should be paid by the outlet, whether the item airs or not.

CHAPTER 3

At the event

On arrival at the television studio or radio station, make the most of it. When I first did *BBC Breakfast*, the best part was having hair and make-up done for free!

Leaving the hotel afterwards, someone even stopped me to ask if I had just been on *BBC Breakfast*! I thought it was hilarious. It was my first time on television, back in 2012!

I wasn't very good at taking photos around the time of the appearance in the early days, though. More recently I have been better at making sure I promote being at the filming/recording, as well as mentioning it on social media after the event.

---

113 Don't worry if the cab doesn't turn up!

If you are travelling up the night before ready for a morning appearance, the company will book a cab for you from the hotel to the station. More often than not it won't turn up! The first couple of times this happens, it can be quite worrying. But actually it is hugely commonplace! Make sure you have the phone number for the station's travel department, so that you can ring it if necessary. Alternatively, ask the hotel reception to get you a taxi, if the booked one has failed to arrive.

114 Offer to arrange your own cab

When I saw how much the cab firm was charging for my taxi to the station, I was shocked. You would think that a large organisation having an account would mean cheaper fares. Far from it. It was twice the price. Knowing that the cabs were also unreliable, I offered to book, pay and include the cost on my invoice. The production company welcomed this. It saves the team some hassle, as well as money, and you can be more confident about getting to the studio and home afterwards!

115 Allow lots of time for travel

This sounds really obvious but it is important! Trains and tubes are still NOT reliable! Allow plenty of time to get to a venue and, just as important, be sure to allow for overrun when thinking about the return time.

If you are travelling from London to Manchester or Leeds for an appearance the following day, do NOT plan to do anything else that day. Turn down the opportunity if it's important for you to be back on time. Very rarely do I get back on time! Once I was home four hours later than I should have been, due to engineering works, broken trains and all sorts!

116 Hair and make-up preparation!

As I mentioned in the introduction, the best part of doing live television for me is having my hair and make-up done!

You normally get your hair done for live television only. Be aware, though, that this is the usual case for BBC, ITV, etc. However, channels such as *GB News* or *TalkTV* might say they have hair and make-up available, but in truth they never get to you! So, go with at least base make-up and they will probably do touch ups.

CHAPTER 3 At the event

117 Don't wear green if a green screen is going to be used

If you are being filmed, you may well be in front of a green screen. For example, when appearing on *ITV Regional News* or a programme where they are interviewing a few experts and want a different background for each of them. Remember not to wear anything green, as you will disappear!

118 Think about cue cards

On magazine style programmes, such as *Morning Live*, you may see presenters using cue cards. This is when people are giving out information as opposed to opinion when interviewed. I used to think that they are used more and looked at far more by presenters given the information than by people who are experts in the area and knew their stuff. Whilst this is generally true, I watched myself on an episode of *Steph's Packed Lunch* and thought "ooooh", as I looked at the cards an awful lot! Despite the fact that it was all my research and knowledge I did want it on cards, out of fear of forgetting something!

Whilst bearing **161 Reflect** in mind, I do find this one difficult to manage. I don't know if I would have forgotten much if I had not asked for so much to go on the cards!

I'm still trying to strike a balance! But then, if you watch these programmes you'll see people looking at their cards all the time! I think it depends on what you think you'll forget, statistics, topical new information, keeping an order (I can do top 5 tips for complaining effectively standing on my head, well I could if I could stand on my head!) but if there are slides going up it's important to get them in the right order! So, think about what will work for you.

In most cases you get to rehearse, which will help. And the people interviewing you are (certainly I have found on these types of programmes) good at their job! This means they will know what you will be saying and will give a prompt in the form of a back-up question, for example.

119 Presenters and production teams are there to help

Keep in mind that everyone wants you to perform at your best. No-one will be there trying to trip you up.

So if you are unsure of anything, ask. They are always going to help, answering questions, discussing anything or putting your mind at rest.

120 Have the Internet ready!

Sometimes, when I have a research call, I'll make sure I have my laptop in front of me. If it's an in-depth call and I haven't had time to research or can't remember everything (I certainly can't remember all the contents of my books!), I'll have relevant page(s) of my blog open to help with answers to any questions.

121 Offer to send information through

If you know you are going to get a call to do the research on what you are going to cover, offer to send some information beforehand. For example, I often cover passenger rights for train delays and cancellations. A researcher will want to ask various questions and they are always mostly the same. So, I send through my post about the topic. This helps the researcher with questions they might want to ask, see the amount of information per question and ultimately save them time, as they can also do some copying and pasting. You can offer to do this after a call, too, of course.

122 Unplug your house phone!

If you're on a mobile phone and you have a house phone, turn it off and vice versa!

CHAPTER 3 At the event

I appeared on the *Vanessa Feltz Show* on *TalkTV*… I was talking about inflation and the price of food. Luckily, they were also interviewing a farmer. I say "luckily", because while I was in contact with the show on my mobile phone, the house phone went. Not only did it ring half a dozen times, but the answering machine kicked in without anybody leaving a message, so it made a horrible noise.

I guessed (correctly) that they had muted me and, of course, they didn't come back to me! Obviously, I apologised, and they were fine, it won't have been the first time something like that has happened. I should have already known about the correct steps to take before a broadcast, just as everyone switches off their mobile phones prior to going on air.

I used to unplug the house phone. I don't know why I stopped doing that! But I'm back to doing it now!

But also think about **159** **Laugh if things go wrong!**

123 Record your radio then transcribe

If you can, use another device to record your radio appearance. Then use a free voice to text program to write everything. Then edit to make a blog post or take snippets to use on social media and refer to the radio appearance where you talked about X, Y and Z. This is a time-efficient way to write more content and use your media coverage.

You can also embed your own videos and/or links to the radio if it's on *BBC Sounds*, for example.

See **231** **Do your own videos**.

124 Be accommodating at the event

Stories and timings change all the time. Especially with live TV and radio. For example, one of the times I was on *Steph's Packed Lunch*, Dr Amos was on to talk about sugar. He did this, but Gemma Collins was also on to talk about incontinence. As he was getting ready to go, they asked him to stay on to do the item with her. They changed their minds on what Gemma was covering and then told him they didn't need him!

This kind of thing happens all the time for all sorts of reasons. Just go with it, and don't worry about it! Take it in your stride and be prepared for change. Make yourself easy to work with!

125 Be honest

This is so important. Saying "I am unsure of that" or "I would have to really think about that for a while before answering" or "That isn't my area of expertise but…" are all better than fumbling or giving out wrong information. It also shows that you are honest and the media teams do not expect you to know everything. This rarely happens but it can do when you haven't been given the likely questions beforehand.

126 Have some questions ready that they could ask

There is no guarantee that an interviewer will use a suggested questions and answers sheet that you might prepare. However, preparing some suitable topics to talk about can help focus you and if the interviewer uses, you'll find it easier. Also if you are talking to a researcher beforehand, this will help make their job easier.

127 Take pics when you are there

If you are on the television or going to a radio station, get photos of you with the presenter(s) and put them on your social media channels. You might also want to use them in your profile banners on social media.

Take pictures outside famous TV buildings, such as the BBC Studios, and share on social media to get people interested in listening/watching before you are on.

Do not do this between takes though! Wait until everything is over and no-one is concentrating on the production!

CHAPTER 3 At the event

128 Enjoy it

Do enjoy the experience. It will be clear to viewers if you don't. If you dislike being on the radio, on television or might have trouble dealing with any trolling after—or have any other negative feelings—then don't do it. Yes, PR is great for your business, yes it does help spread the word, yes it is free… but. If you don't enjoy it and you are uncomfortable, it isn't going to work and no PR is worth a kick to your mental health.

There is nothing anywhere that says you MUST do PR! And if not you, perhaps someone else in your company might want to appear instead?

129 Always be aware!

Always think the camera is on you, so you don't do 'resting bitch face' waiting for your turn to speak…like I did for 3 full seconds on *BBC Breakfast* or do the Gordon Brown 'switch-on smile'.

130 Being controversial on air

It may seem scary, but don't worry about saying something that people might think is a 'bit out there' or that will get people arguing. Whether you have thought about it being controversial or not or even a joke. For example Anupa Roper is a Body Image Educator and bestselling Children's Author of *Sparrowlegs*.

Anupa appeared on *Talk Radio* with Kevin O'Sullivan to discuss the 'fat shaming' of Tilly Ramsay. Kevin agreed with Anupa but said that there is freedom of speech and fat shaming can't be outlawed. Anupa quipped that "maybe there should be a law!" From that comment the *Express* covered the story "Activist calls for 'fat shaming' to be made a crime as debate erupts over free speech".

See **60** **Be controversial in mainstream media,** **190** **Be controversial in your press release** and **239** **Be controversial on social media**.

131 Be ready to disagree

Sometimes you may be on the radio or TV with another guest, talking alternative views, which is a good opportunity to show your debating skills and keep calm whilst passionate about your opinions, etc. Sometimes things may not go to plan. Or your plan!

For example, I was once on the radio and the other guest said that he didn't agree with something I had said. That would have been fine, except for the fact that I didn't say it. Unfortunately, the presenter did not come back to me and the item finished after the other guest had spoken. At the time I was extremely annoyed. However, one needs to remind oneself that two seconds after the item everyone would have forgotten what we said anyway, unless perhaps it was a piece of advice they wanted to follow immediately!

So, just let it go, use the fact that you're in the media and bear in mind that possibly somebody was sitting there listening who shouted at the radio to correct the other person, too!

132 Give the presenter a product

If your business has a product you sell that is not expensive, take some along to the location. Give them to team members. If you give one to the person who booked/chatted with you, they will be delighted. How often do you think they get anything?! It means they will remember you, too.

After giving him a copy, Dominic Littlewood tried to get my book into *The One Show* segment I was involved in, but they edited it out for the broadcast! But it does go to show that some of the nice guys out there will try and put things forward, too.

Also sometimes people put on X (formerly Twitter) or Instagram "Thank you for x", which is perfect PR!

133 Recording TV appearances

Put 'catch-up' links to your appearances on your social media channels. Viewers like to watch clips if they missed you first time round and when the media come looking they will see that you are a safe pair of hands.

134 Wear different clothes

I do not advocate only ever wearing something once! However, think long term, as if you make a showreel some time later, you don't want to be seen in the same outfit twice. Otherwise, it may look like you have done fewer appearances than you have if images are similar, particularly as you will probably repeat some shows in your first showreel. It also can come across as dull or you have a 'uniform' so try and mix up what you have!

In my showreel I also seem to have accidentally had a few different hairstyles, too, but I couldn't help going grey and I do like the hair and make-up being done for me on live shows!

135 Have notes

Make notes, even some key points that you could read out if you are being interviewed over the phone (but don't sound like you are reading!). I do this all the time, usually with excerpts from a related blog post. It helps get the key points across, keeps you focussed and means you will be less likely to forget anything! You can also write notes to take with you on your journey to help get them fixed in your head.

136 Offer ideas

If you have built up a good rapport with the person who booked you, ask if they would like ideas for future coverage from you. Some magazine shows are open to you sending ideas. Just be aware though that sometimes they will have had the idea or simply use someone else. I have got work through giving ideas and also seen other people cover my ideas!

137 Don't give out business cards!

I've never seen this happen on any media production in which I've participated. But Marta Zaczkowska, a Waxing expert, encountered this whilst taking part in the *Stand Up To Cancer* live show on *Channel 4*.

She was asked to participate in Joe Lycett's "Guess Who" game and was stunned to see another participant handing out business cards to celebrities! Don't do this!

It really is NOT the done thing. It will come across as ignorant and very naive.

It's all about building relationships (see much of this book!). If someone is interested in what you do then they will ask for your contact details. Marta commented that it was very bizarre. "I overheard people behind the scenes mentioning that such behaviour could prevent them from being invited back in the future."

138 Be yourself

In the famous words of Oscar Wilde "Be yourself, everyone else is already taken". Remember that people buy from people. Your product could be the best thing since sliced bread but viewers or listeners will warm to genuine and credible people. If you try and be something you are not it will come across and it just won't work.

Producers who book experts want to see genuine people and often when you have done one piece of media, another outlet may pick up on you but only if you come across as genuine.

But, most importantly, there is one exception to this! Don't ever swear live on TV or radio, even if you do normally use bad language to punctuate what you say!! One of my worst fears is for me to do that by accident!

139 Don't worry about being cut!

However long you are filmed for, do not think that it will all be used! I remember when I first started being filmed that I thought I must have been rubbish because they cut so much! But it's not the case. Frequently they will ask you to say similar things in different ways so they can edit accordingly, depending on time available. They always want more footage than they need, so they have a choice.

Other times, particularly for short films, and as I'm now more experienced things are often quicker and finished in fewer takes.

Half an hour filming may well go down to under a minute on air!

Also other things happen resulting in different priorities. I was filmed for hours for the *Glasgow Willy Wonka experience—what happened* documentary. But the production company secured the Willy Wonka event organiser for an interview and they had to turn round the editing in just a few days. This meant that a lot had to be cut and they didn't have the usual discussions about what to use. I think I made 6 seconds! But even then, I used this fact to still push out a joke about my quick appearance with a picture of the coverage on all my social media platforms, to start conversations and gain more engagement.

CHAPTER 4

Getting paid

How and when do you start to get paid for your TV or radio appearances?

There is no definitive answer to this! There are some examples throughout the book of ways to get paid for your work or story but the information below is about getting paid for being an expert. **CHAPTER 1 Starting to get publicity in mainstream media** gives some examples of how you can get paid for magazine work in the sections **27 Feature Me**, **28 Make the Headlines** and **32 Sell your story**.

Many years ago I recorded for *BBC General News Service* (now *Central News Service*), in an appearance lasting two hours. Local BBC stations choose if they want to join in and so you appear on whichever channels opt to take part, for about five minutes with each station. I did it because it was good PR. The woman who booked me asked if I did this for a living? I said "Well, I'd like to, if I got paid for it!" She said "We can pay you if you would like". Simple! From that point on I have always asked for payment.

You may have hoped that this chapter would have been longer! However, it is the track record of PR work that gets you into the position of being able to request payment and once you are there there's no special magic formula for getting paid!

As you build experience it will become easier to ask for and charge a fee. However, my first media experience was an opinion piece for the free local paper, the second was *BBC Breakfast* and the third was on *BBC Radio 5*, for which I was paid. So, there are no rules about when you can start being paid for your expertise. In addition, there are other ways to get paid for your story too.

140 Ask for a fee

Once you've done a few appearances as an expert in an area related to your business, then ask for a fee. They can only say "no" and will more often say "yes"!

BBC Breakfast pay a "disturbance fee" for most appearances, so always ask!

I say "What is the fee?", rather than "Is there a fee?" This shows that you know your worth and that you are used to being paid for your work.

141 Know when to start saying "no"

Over the last couple of years I've chosen to turn down some work that doesn't pay, unless I feel like it. Once you start getting paid, you can still do the free stuff, as it is PR that costs you nothing. But once you've started appearing frequently as a paid expert, you then have to weigh up whether it's worth it, or not.

For example, when I was first doing radio, it was good PR and I was able to say I've done this, that or the other. However, after a few years of appearances on one station, I wasn't selling any more books and didn't get any more social media likes/follows, so I decided it was no longer worth my time.

Further down the line, the question arises: are you getting any value from doing PR for free? Or it could be that all PR is good and/or that you may want to be heard on your local stations. *BBC London* is my local station and I often appear there, as it has a fairly large audience, too.

There is an argument that you are still reaching people, who may be disengaged from the mainstream outlets, so you will have to weigh up the pros and cons for yourself.

CHAPTER 4 Getting paid

142 What if there's no fee on offer?

Quite simply, push for full-on promotion of you and your brand! Most, if not all outlets, will allow it. Some outlets are brilliant for this. You don't have to feel like you are pushing, as many presenters, particularly on local radio will often ask "Tell everyone where they can find you". The *BBC Radio* local channels, aware of not paying, will usually give your business a good shout out. You can suggest how you would like to be introduced and ask if they can mention anything relevant.

143 Negotiate

Okay, so this is horrible, but it can be done! Most TV and radio outlets have a set fee for non-celebrity experts. But when you have been going for a few years, it is worth trying to increase your rate.

For example, I have even done this with one *BBC Radio 4* programme, but on the whole, the BBC will be really hard! However, one of the news channels is very much more flexible and I've negotiated higher amounts for doing five minutes on a weekend, for instance, and by saying that "X paid me Y on Z show". My experience, and the outlet's lack of fee consistency across programmes and experts, helps a lot when working for them!

I would recommend negotiating only after you have appeared on the specific show a few times, as you will feel more comfortable (!) and also more likely to get it because they like, know and trust you.

144 Agents

An agent is the person who can represent you in negotiating the rate of pay with the media outlet. The agent will take a commission, usually between 15% and 20%.

Yes, I have an agent. But! It takes a lot of work to get one and it doesn't necessarily mean that they will get work for you. Unless you get lucky by being a reality TV star and are snapped up. You'll need a lot of work under your belt to bag an agent. A potential agent will want to see a variety of TV and radio experience, demonstrating your expertise, as well as a professionally made "showreel". A showreel is a video about two to three minutes long showcasing a selection of your media appearances. You should include a variety of outlets and demonstrate different areas of your expertise.

My first showreel had mainly radio and looking back on it wasn't that great but it was a start! Then I had one that was much better and my Showreel has received a lot of compliments, for Tom Stanhope, a professional video producer who put it together as well as the content!

Many years ago, I approached more than 50 agents, seeking representation! I managed to get two offers! I researched one of them a little further, as in a past life he had been a successful comedian, but found out he had become extremely racist in his "humour", so didn't want to work with him!

I then found an agent who actually did get me five minutes on *Talk Radio* (unpaid) and a publishing contract for my first book. However, when I did my due diligence, I found that even though they were offering 40% royalties (that's an extremely high percentage for a book), I was still financially better off staying self-published, as I was selling more books than their current best-seller!

They annoyed me along the way, so I looked for another agent!

I had kept a record of agents that I'd contacted and if they had replied. I went back to any that sounded slightly positive in any way!

I met a few. One of them completely wasted my time, as her reason for not taking me was that she already had a consumer person! Watch out for that if it's a small agency (and it will be, if you're just starting out). You'll see that very few have more than one expert in a specialist area, unless it's an agency dedicated to that sector. Another offered me speaking gigs but at that time I wasn't brave enough to agree!

I contacted my current agent, who had been positive and encouraging in the first refusal. An updated showreel and more work got me a meeting and a contract with him. But even if you do get past all the hurdles of trying to find an agent, it does not mean that you will necessarily get more work! Agents rarely go touting for business for those at the less experienced end because it's not financially viable in terms of their time. My agent did try to get me onto a few outlets on which I hadn't already appeared at the time and secured my first *One Show* appearance, as well as another stint at *Rip-Off Britain*.

CHAPTER 4 Getting paid

But at the present time, agents focus on where the money is! To be fair, mine is always there for advice and to listen to a rant! And whenever I don't know what to charge, he will advise and do the necessary negotiating.

It's really not worth spending time and effort looking for an agent until you have a good variety of work that you can demonstrate, including in a showreel. Don't repeat anything in the showreel, as it will simply appear that don't have enough material. In my last one, I really struggled to cut!

It's also worth noting that most people will stop watching after a couple of minutes.

However, the influencer route is becoming more common for securing an agent. Maddy Alexander Grout is a money specialist who started sharing her money tips on TikTok.

A year after starting her TikTok account Maddy had gained 10,000 followers and within 18 months she had 60,000. She began by covering how to save money, spend less and make more money. Just three months in, one of her videos went viral. She appeared on the *BBC News* website talking about buying cheaper vegetables. She tried to ensure that she gave value in every post and used 6-8 hashtags, many of which were not too popular. She created her own unique hashtag which at the point of publishing has over 24 million views: #madaboutmoneyofficial

Maddy heard that some TikTok creators had launched a Christmas single and thought it was a great idea. Following most of them, she made a couple of videos to help promote it. Their PR woman commented on one of the *Mad About Money* videos and so Maddy started following her, too!

After going viral again with some harsh comments, see **154 Ignore the trolls on online articles** and **155 Ignore the trolls on social media too**, the PR woman messaged Maddy to say she was doing a really good job and not to be disheartened. She discussed the other influencers she represented and offered to take on Maddy.

145 Invoicing

Make sure to ask the person who books you for details of the invoicing procedure. Do you need to send an invoice or do they have 'self-billing' in place, which means that they prepare the invoice paperwork and then send you the payment automatically? What are their terms for payment? Do you need to register your bank details with them? Who is the contact in case of queries?

The BBC, for example, will allocate you a "contributor number" and you can just use that each time you are on one of their shows.

Keep an eye on payments, as certain outlets are notorious for needing to be chased!

See **112 Don't worry about cancellations!**

CHAPTER 5

After your appearances

When you have finished your media appearance, don't just leave it there! There's more mileage to be had than just reaching the audience on television or radio.

A recent discussion in Lightbulb involved journalists talking about people who had appeared on TV/radio and then not 'shared' the experience on social media. It does not make sense. Why do the PR and then not share it? Some people said they didn't share on their personal social media feeds because they thought their followers wouldn't be interested! Then they will scroll past if they aren't interested! Friends will engage and help your reach and possibly share, too!

You want to be sharing everywhere possible.

146 Follow up appearances on social media

Follow up everything in your social media: tag the outlet before you are on, announcing your appearance, and then after, thanking the person with whom you appeared and the outlet. Put the link to where people can find more information, if appropriate. Outlets rarely retweet or share but it still gets the message out there.

If it's an opinion piece, ask for social media users' views on the issue to get engagement with your media piece before and after, providing different views on it. This can be particularly good for getting more visibility on LinkedIn, for example.

In August 2023, Etsy hit the news about its move to withhold 75% of some sellers' money for 45 days. There was huge backlash. Liz Barclay from the Small Business Commission had already been trying to work with Etsy on the issue and the problems it was causing for UK businesses. But nothing is as strong as media pressure and they did back down within days of *Sky News Online* and *BBC News* covering the story. In that time an *Etsy Reserve Strike* group had been set up on Facebook and Susan Bonnar had pitched in Lightbulb about The British Craft House (TBCH).

An article on *Sky News* titled "What's happening with Etsy and its reserve system?" was published on the Thursday, my press release "Etsy hassles - UK company offers an alternative for makers and crafters" went onto the blog on Friday and my interview with Susan Bonnar, founder of The British Craft House on *The Complaining Cow Consumer Show* on *East London Radio* was published on the Saturday.

The following Wednesday, Amazon hit the news for withholding money for Amazon sellers causing serious cashflow issues for sellers. Following on from my press release sent a few days before regarding Etsy I was asked to talk about the issues on the *Jeremy Vine Show* on *BBC Radio 2*. (See **188 Realistic expectations**).

In discussing how consumers can support small UK businesses, I mentioned going to sellers' own websites and alternatives such as TBCH.

Susan really grasped the need to use this coverage to increase traffic to her site which resulted in more applications from sellers and more sales for the sellers.

Her inclusion in the *Sky News* article was from seeing a tweet by a *Sky News* journalist—see **11 #JournoRequest**.

On the back of this she posted a pitch in Lightbulb—see **25 Facebook Lightbulb group**—and got picked up for a press release and radio show with me and a further radio show for her local station.

She says that for her social media post with the link to my article she made sure it had a nice graphic that people would share and that the graphics were the right size for each social media platform. With Tweets she scheduled them to go out again throughout each day. She shared to both her personal and business pages, as everyone is a customer! She has a sellers' hub, so she displayed the links there and asked visitors to comment and share. She is fully aware that Facebook posts get more visibility if you 'wow' or 'love' and write comments of five words or more.

CHAPTER 5 After your appearances

Now this took even more time but undoubtedly helped drive traffic. On every post she replied to every comment, on every platform, going in a loop and around again! You need to do that for days! She says "It's exhausting and often requires wine and or chocolate!" Yes, we do have a lot in common, it would appear!

Susan's customers are mainly on Facebook and Instagram but when it had all calmed down a bit she also posted on Threads, LinkedIn and TikTok.

Keeping it in the public eye is key, as is staying on top of shares, especially to comment and give thanks, but to also follow up any questions that might be on the shared post!

Susan also tagged me in a lot of posts to thank me which meant I reacted, commented and shared her posts, as well as my own to drive traffic to my site. Having been on the *Jeremy Vine Show* many times over the years I don't now get many followers on social media or visits to the site (at least I hope that's the reason!) But the social media activity sent more traffic and I got more followers, especially on Instagram. This shows the power of social media if you use your publicity wisely.

You have to be on it!

See **274 Milk it**.

It is tiring if you get a run like this but the results are well worth it. See **162 Wind down**.

147 Follow up comments in articles on social media

Make sure you share any links to articles in which you are quoted on all your social media platforms. You can do this more than once. Also consider sharing the journalist's tweet, so that they know too. Say something simple to go with it, such as "Please to contribute to this article…"

See **149 Put up your coverage on your website** regarding sharing images.

148 Thank journalists appropriately

Don't be all gushing or post "Thank you so much I appreciate it, blah blah blah" nonsense! Remember, you are helping them out too. It's a partnership. You can say privately "Thank you and please don't hesitate to ask me for comments on xyz in the future." It looks ridiculous on social media. You could say something like "Pleased to contribute to this article on…"

I wrote about Leah Turner in the *Metro*. See 90 **Think of a journey**. It was a relatively long and detailed post and gave her business quite a shout out. I was delighted for Leah to hear that she had made many sales and a lot of money.

She sent me a beautiful bouquet of flowers! And I certainly wouldn't expect this from my case studies! And in fact, when some people have asked for my address to send something I've refused to give it because at the end of the day I got paid for the article. But if you feel that someone has done a really good job for you and you have truly benefited then gestures like this can make a journalist's day but certainly a "Thank you" is essential.

Jill Foster counsels "If you're happy with the story—and most people are if they work well with the journalist—it's always worth saying 'thank you' and then staying in touch. Journalists move around and work for different editors and publications so if another story opportunity comes up and they remember you as a reliable, interesting person, they're more likely to come back to you."

Also a note of caution: I know of a few female journalists who find it very uncomfortable when men are too enthusiastic in emails and messages. Don't fawn! Journalists won't like you any more for it!

149 Put up your coverage on your website

The media coverage works as testimonials, too, so continue to use them as you would with any other reference. Do not take pictures of print and use them without permission, as there are copyright rules about this. But you can link and use your own pictures and those for which you do have permission.

I used to routinely put up every piece of media I had done on my website and date it. The list got ridiculously long and went back years, so there does come a point where it makes sense to limit this to "As seen on/in", with links.

150 Logos

Once you have a few appearances under your belt, use the logos and "As seen on", however small, on your website and other publicity material. It shows that you are a safe pair of hands when editors go searching for contributors, as well as doing the PR for you. Although, strictly speaking, permission should be given, you will see there are thousands of them all over the Internet used for promotion and this is widely accepted. The worst that could happen is an outlet asking you to take it down but this is very unlikely.

151 Use your products

If you sell products, send a sample with a witty or thought-provoking message to the media person with whom you spoke. This is particularly good if there is some in-joke you had and say "get in contact if you ever need someone to talk about xyz". I have not done this so much with local media but it certainly worked on some occasions with national outlets. My first book is particularly useful and always gratefully received!

152 Follow up with the outlet

Contact the person who booked you/you worked with after the package goes out and say it was good working with them, thank them and say that you hope to do so again. Give them a follow on social media too. If they follow you back you'll obviously be in their feed but also it's a nice thing to do! As a journalist I certainly appreciate a follow.

153 Follow the production team on social media

Most people follow the programme they have just been on but (a) they rarely follow back and (b) it's a social media person/team running the account. Follow production team members you have met. If they follow you back then you are kept in their feed.

154 Ignore the trolls on online articles

You'll hear this often from journalists. If you appear in an article as a case study, the comments can be horrendous on some outlets. It's just not worth looking, some people are simply foul.

When you get an article about you published online, do not read the comments, often referred to as 'below the line'. I'll repeat that, do not read the comments. You may well be tempted. But just don't do it. You might get the odd nice comment but if you look at any article about anybody online, there are always comments coming from a place of jealousy, spite and just plain old trolling. There is no reason why an article about you will be any different. It is important to just use the article for PR. It will also not do your credibility any good to respond.

I remember writing for *This Is Money*, "As Sainsbury's turns away a guide dog, the CONSUMER FIGHTBACK column reveals your rights under the Equality Act", which was about Sainsbury's not allowing a woman into the store with a guide dog.

Obviously, Sainsbury's apologised, gave training to the member of staff who had refused entry and made a donation to Guide Dogs. I scanned the comments and couldn't believe that someone had actually said that the dog should not have been allowed in. NINETEEN people liked the comment. Given the fact that this would be a breach of the Equality Act and that guide dogs are highly trained, this was a pretty ignorant and nasty comment.

Some people will find any angle to be horrible to others.

CHAPTER 5 After your appearances

155 Ignore the trolls on social media too

I recommend a similar approach to **154 Ignore the trolls on online articles** on social media. "Mute" and "Block" are powerful buttons. Use them to ignore and forget the trolls.

Responding to trolls, whether directly or in a passive aggressive manner online, is tempting but is a complete waste of your time and energy. Years ago I used to do this. I'm feisty, opinionated and argumentative, so why wouldn't I?! There was never any point however, as no troll wants a reasoned discussion.

It's also good to remember that if you are getting trolls you are on the right path and doing well. There will always be people who are having a worse time with trolls than you. Lisa Johnson had such a bad time with a troll who defamed her that she took her case to court and won. She has thousands and thousands of followers and is extremely successful and consequently also has a lot of trolls. A few years ago, when I was getting more than my fair share of trolls, including people I had previously helped, I listened to one of Lisa's podcasts titled "How To Deal With People Who Treat you Badly Online". If you are getting trolls or even before you start your journey, I would thoroughly recommend listening to this. It really helped me put a different spin on how and what I felt towards my trolls.

Kate Hall, Founder of The Full Freezer and author, discovered the benefit of this when an Instagram reel she shared went viral. Despite the content achieving 44,700 likes, and Kate gaining 20,000 new followers, it was the negative comments that stuck with her. Making the decision to block and move on has allowed her to continue to share her valuable content without being held back by those who simply don't 'get it' or don't want to.

Once I made the decision to stop responding, and then stop looking at anyone I had muted or blocked, I felt so much better. Resolve to do this from the start of your PR journey. If you unwisely join in, other people see a spat too, it can escalate and ultimately reflect badly on you. So, when you see a message from a potential troll, just ignore it. And if you get 'helpful' people sending you screenshots, ask them politely not to send you them in future!

Occasionally you may find that a troll apologises, but it is very rare and usually for damage limitation (such as was suggested in the case of Chrissy Teigen when she apologised for online bullying). If a troll later apologises it, of course, depends on you and the circumstances as to whether you accept it!

See also **59** **Use your vulnerabilities**, **158** **Ignore the competition** and **270** **Try not to correct other experts!**

156 Be prepared to not be fully happy!

When journalists write a piece about you, it is very rare for them to give you editorial control. Some will, some will want to and not be allowed and some just won't! So, remember that you may well not like everything written about you.

It's usually down to the editor when there's a change that you don't like. For example, I often get coverage that says I "...make a career of complaining..." or "...make money from complaining..." or that it is my profession! This is not accurate. I only get refunds when legally entitled to my money back or the money back for other people. That is not a career, nor is it my profession. But editors quite often like this kind of spin in the title headline. I would still share and list such an article because it is coverage!

Judi Hampton is a positivity consultant and the founder of Look See & Feel Amazing. She was delighted to be asked to feature in a women's magazine about how magnets had changed her life. The magazine edited her story to read like a love story. She said that nothing was really wrong but it wasn't her. Judi asked the journalist, who explained that their readers expected the articles to be written in a certain way! Things she didn't agree with were "I waved my kids off to school, then once their backs were turned I swallowed some painkillers" which was not true, as she never hid anything from them! And her husband Kevin, 49, had been a saint! That one made her laugh, as that wasn't true either! It's rare for journalists to really embellish the facts and you can attempt to mitigate, as above. But try to see the positive, even if you aren't entirely happy with the coverage.

Judi has since given presentations about what really happened and what was embellished.

See **159** **Laugh if things go wrong and use to your advantage**.

Also remember that the journalist is not responsible for the headline. It may

CHAPTER 5 After your appearances

well be that you don't like the headline and/or feel it doesn't reflect your story, but editors and sub editors know what to write to get the clicks on the article.

If you are unhappy with how you have been portrayed in an article you can always talk about it in a social media video/post which is another way of showing off your PR.

You can also get 'copy shock' when you see your own words in print for the first time! Check that you did say them before telling anyone it isn't what you said!

157 Remind people you exist!

If you have been quoted a few times or been on/in an outlet a few times and they haven't used you for a while, you can always drop them a line to say you are still around if they should need a comment. Hooking this to something currently in the news can be helpful in prompting a positive response. I have done this a number of times and it often gets me back onto various radio outlets.

158 Ignore the competition

Everyone will always have competition in whatever their specialist field. Some will copy you, some will have very little integrity, some will just be plain rubbish! Others you should work with. Concentrate your efforts on demonstrating the skills, knowledge, experience and personality that you have, rather than criticising the competition.

Trying to denigrate other experts in your sector will make you look daft and if journalists are following both of you on X (formerly Twitter), imagine what they will think? I had a troll 'expert' do this and two journalists messaged me to say they saw it as a clear case of sour grapes!

Another 'expert' incorrectly tried to correct a large well-known consumer organisation. He made himself look very silly! I know people in that organisation just laughed and ignored him. He also lost any possibility of future collaborations with them.

Where possible, work in partnership and help each other. If they don't want to do this, that says a lot more about them than about you.

Whilst 'competition' that doesn't want to work with you should be ignored, definitely work with others in your field if you can. A rising tide raises all ships.

See **78** Recommend other experts.

159 Laugh if things go wrong and use to your advantage

It won't always go right every time. I was recently on *The Jeremy Vine Show* on *BBC Radio 2*, when my mobile phone rang. I thought I had turned it off. Then the doorbell went and the dog started barking. I thought I had lost my thread, but when I listened to the recording it was OK and when I joked about it on social media people said it was fine. So, if something does go wrong, it will give you reason to write something else to show your PR and that you have a sense of humour!

Do this when things are outside of your control too. For example when I was interviewed by Jacob Rees-Mogg on *GB News*, they put my name on his image. I used the image on all my social media with various posts, made a funny video as my first TikTok and changed my profile picture on Facebook which all gained a lot of engagement and followers.

See **156** Be prepared to not be fully happy!

160 Monitor the effects of coverage

This can be tedious and I'm not great at it, but it probably would have helped in some decision making a few years ago.

After each piece of coverage, analyse the metrics and keep a record. What was the outlet? How much coverage did you/your brand generate? How much social media coverage from the outlet, from which platforms, from what type of social media engagement? How many additional visits to your website and how many sales and other opportunities? Ultimately, what drove traffic to where and what was the outcome?

CHAPTER 5 After your appearances

Monitoring the metrics in this way will show you who engages with your content and where they do it. It will help develop other areas of your business, as well as where to focus your PR efforts. See also **3 ▶ The 7 touch points of marketing**.

You may need to tweak your PR plan as you go. See **4 ▶ Read the book and make a plan!**

Maddy Alexander Grout monitors her analytics and recreates what works. After three months of analysing her statistics on TikTok she went viral and has gone viral many times since. She looks at views, time of posting, where the audience is located, their age and how many comments there are. This all helps to understand what type of content reaches the largest and target audience, and when.

161 Reflect

If you want and you feel able, look back at your performance. But know that you will be your own worst critic! So, only review the recording if you can promise yourself that you won't be too self-critical! Maybe you want to check "how you sit" (I do this and tell myself every time that I lean forward too much but don't always remember to do anything about it! So, these things are not crucial). Or maybe you want to critique how you answer the questions. Remember, you will always think you could have said more or in a better way. It is natural to be harsh on yourself. I do it all the time, I still get asked back, even though I still often wish I said more/different things!

But it can be good to see if there was anything you worried about whilst you were speaking or straight after was justified. For example, I often think I 'ummed' and 'erred' too much. I do, but not too much. So, it can put your mind at rest too.

And like anything else, things get better with practice.

Dr Marianne Trent, a Clinical Psychologist, tells me:

"It's understandable that, when watching ourselves back, we might do so with a critical eye. An awareness of ourself and how others might see us is part of the human condition. If barriers, blocks or alternate messages come to you whilst you're watching yourself on replay or re-reading your published work, then it's useful stuff to work through.

Given that we want you to be wildly successful, then it is advantageous to develop your tolerance so that you can do more publicity rather than letting your thoughts, feelings and fears keep you small. There's evidence that sometimes our own self-critic can stop us from even trying to do the things to which we aspire. It can therefore be helpful to try and rally your 'compassionate other' and try to connect to what your 'perfect nurturer' might want for you in this moment. For example, if it was your best friend, they would want you to feel proud, know that you had done a good job, that you came across as credible and that it's wonderful you've been able to share your knowledge with others. It's okay that this might take time, but it is safe for you to be visible and to promote yourself and your business whilst helping others at the same time.

You don't deserve to suffer but you do deserve to be successful. So, if, over time, you experience negative, critical or hostile personal reactions to your own work, working through it with a qualified psychologist or performance coach might be useful."

162 Wind down

When you start doing media appearances, especially in the early days, you may find you are excited and hyper.

You may also be keen to talk about your experience, so do it with friends who want to hear. Sometimes meeting with other guests is more entertaining than your own media appearance! I know I have really enjoyed getting the inside stories of programmes and their presenters, so that's what I like to share! Whether it's Dr Amos talking about what really went on in *The Traitors* or Alexis Conran discussing scams or Kerry Katona musing on her life or members of the public telling their stories, they all give me something I want to share!

Dr Trent says:

"In order to get out there and 'do a thing' we may need to increase our arousal levels. This might mean that we then feel more wired, alert and responsive and that our thoughts and words flow more easily during this time.

However, once our performance time is over, we'll likely need to decompress and lower our arousal state back down the window of tolerance. Due to the way that our hormones are impacted in this whole process, it's totally normal if you might also feel a bit exhausted and spacey for some time afterwards, too. This is a normal response to the coming down from the hormones leaving our system.

Take care of yourself. Try to do some slow, rhythmic breathing, make some time and space for quiet. If you've been very social or on for a long period of time, you might well also find it useful to factor in a few days of 'down time' with family or friends who will take care of you afterwards!"

163 Use national in local...

If you get some national publicity coverage, tell your local paper, if you have one. They may run a story on you about the coverage you are getting on national media, whether it's television, radio or press.

164 Keep things in perspective

Doing the PR stuff can be fun and whilst you may not be paying for it, don't let it take up too much of your time. If you neglect your customers, your business will suffer. You need your customers to support you in saying how great you are. You want your customers to do some of your marketing, so look after them well.

CHAPTER 6

Building your media contact list

A media contact list contains the details of a variety of people working in the press, radio and TV who may be able to give you PR opportunities. You can use this list to send press releases and keep in contact with your chosen group.

This chapter is about creating and developing a mailing list through which you can keep in touch with the media. Maintaining your contact list is time consuming and relentless. However, the actions you can take to build this are key to ensuring that you are regularly in the media.

I started my contact list after undertaking a few pieces of PR. It is constantly being updated and changed but the work has been worthwhile in securing much (now paid) work.

It may take you a lot of time to collect names for future contact. Remember that it is your time and effort that is being expended. You wouldn't (shouldn't!) give away your expertise for free. People have to pay for your knowledge and so that goes for your hard work on gathering and collating media contacts, too. Anyone can follow the advice in this book. When people ask me for my contacts I say "no". They were gained through hard work, so are not something to give away for free. It's not the done thing and your contact won't thank you for it.

Also, if people haven't done the preparation work and don't know what they are doing in their approach and why, then any email will just get ignored. I get requests like this from individuals starting out on their PR journey who think it's just a matter of contacting people! They often think their service is unique when it clearly is not, so they need to do the work on angles. In addition, your contacts, who are already inundated with emails, will not thank you for passing on their details! Please don't do this as you will not do yourself any favours with your contacts! You might be breaching General Data Protection Regulation (GDPR) if you passed on details!

Remember if you pay a PR person/agency to get you coverage that saves you time, you are paying for their knowledge, expertise and contacts built up over time. They wouldn't give it away for free, so neither should you.

165 Build a press release list

This is where the hard work starts! Don't worry about only having one or two contacts in your list and how it seems to grow so slowly. It certainly will grow if you put the work in.

Set up a spreadsheet and start the process! Along the columns, suggested headings would be "Name", "Email address", "Outlet", "Role", "Personal" and "Notes". As you build your spreadsheet, put the details in accordingly. Under the "personal" put a "Y" or "N". You can then filter for people whom you want to message individually. However, I started this long before thinking of using a system for managing mailing lists! For example, Mailchimp is free for your first 500 contacts. That's ideal while you start.

Be aware of your responsibilities under the General Data Protection Regulation (GDPR). To join a mailing list, members must opt in. However, there are some exemptions to GDPR rules and journalistic purposes is one of them.

If you are keeping personal data for any business reason you must pay a Data Protection fee to be registered with the Information Commissioner's Office.

Whenever mailing to your press list you must provide an option allowing people to unsubscribe.

166 Watch journalist movements

You may have to demonstrate that you are a journalist to be able to sign up for helpful daily emails with movements of journalists through **23** **Response Source** for free. So, if a journalist of interest is in your business sector, add their name to your list and then work out their email address(es). Don't worry,

CHAPTER 6 Building your media contact list

I'm going to tell you how to do that, too.

Similarly you can do the same with CISION.

167 X (formerly known as Twitter)

Do the same on X as you do with LinkedIn. Follow people, looking out for their email addresses, which can be found in the profile of many journalists on that social media platform.

168 Email addresses

Keep the email addresses that you get through **23** **Response Source** in their trial.

169 Local contacts

Find out the email addresses for local radio stations and local papers. When it comes to sending out press releases you can personalise these to say "Local" with details about the local connection and where you are based. This gives them an added reason to book you/use your press release. It can also provide you with an edge when dealing with local and regional journalists.

170 Online email addresses

Many articles will discuss stories and seek more people to contact them with their own experiences. For example, there was a consumer story about customers of a supermarket being searched and two email addresses were provided, asking people if they had been affected. This gave me two email addresses to add to my press release email list.

171 LinkedIn contacts

Do searches for producers, researchers, news people in general and in the sectors that interest you. Some profiles will contain the person's email address, some will have them in the contact info if they connect with you or try and work out the email format, for example: *firstname.secondname@bbc.co.uk*

It doesn't always work when people have the same name as someone else in the organisation but it's certainly a good way to make a start.

CHAPTER 7

Sending out press releases

Press releases aren't as effective as they once were 10-20 years ago (much more is undertaken in networking and social media than before) but it is still a place where lots of the magic happens. There are many reasons for sending out press releases.

I send out press releases on a regular basis, finding that topical issues work well because production teams always need people to comment on them. The trick is to be quick off the mark.

You could start to reap the benefits of issuing press releases as soon as you send your first one or it may take a few goes. Whatever happens, you'll be getting your name out there in front of the relevant journalists.

Start to send out press releases to your list of contacts. Get into the frame of mind of topical and trending stories. Use your expertise to comment on relevant subjects in the media but be quick whilst the matter remains current.

172 Understand what a press release is and isn't

A press release isn't a pitch or a feature. It's an announcement about a new product or service or an opinion on something topical.

Put yourself in the mind of your journalist/reader audience and ask yourself if other people will be interested in what you're writing about? Strike an emotion.

Journalists like their readers to be moved. Is it new, innovative, sad, happy, frustrating? Perhaps it touches on a nerve and so will provoke a reaction? Ideally, you want to move people to feel something to which they can relate.

Journalists receive hundreds of press releases every single day. Make sure you have a good catchy title. Something like "Top 5 x" works well.

"My son ate an elephant and turned blue" rather than "My son ate an elephant sweet and his tongue went blue" is going to grab attention. Think clickbait and get the most important information out in that first paragraph.

173 Choose a title carefully

Clickbait is text, or a picture with text, that entices you to "click" and read the link. Often clickbait can mislead you into thinking you are going to see something shocking. For example, "Martin Lewis sends back OBE". In actual fact it was because he had to do so in order to have it "upgraded" to a CBE.

"x number of ways to do…", "xyz revealed…" are examples of titles that you think will hook people in. However, use these carefully. Although you want to engage a journalist's interest and you want the email opened, you do not want to mislead them.

174 Appeal to the journalist by making it easy to see why they should use your press release

Keep it simple and interesting. You want people to identify with the contents and for it to be significant to them. For a journalist or editor to be interested, ask yourself the "So what?" and "Why now?" questions which your press release needs to address as to why the contents are important and significant at this moment in time. Then answer them in the press release.

CHAPTER 7 Sending out press releases

175 Focus on impact and audience

Having thought about the "So what?" and "Why now?" questions to initially appeal to the journalist, remember that they don't really care about you or your business unless you bring value to them in some way. They do care about what their audience feels and the impact of the story. Thinking about emotions is good. Will the audience wish it were them, think it is them, be pleased it's not them or for them?

176 Press release templates

You can search on the Internet for free press release templates. I'd advise if you do this, to get one from a PR company that clearly has a lot of work and knows how to write one that is effective. They will likely be offering it free to get your email address and put you on a list from which you can unsubscribe. But the tips below will help you put a press release together.

177 Structure the press release

Summarise the story in a sub title.

Press releases should be relatively short, ideally less than one page of A4 in font size 12, just a few short paragraphs. 400 words is ideal. Write to hook the recipient in from the start. The most important information should be in the first paragraph.

This should be followed by the background, context, details and any quotes. Then any statistics and facts to support the main angle.

Subheadings can work, too, if your release is on the longer side. Put these in bold for easier reading.

Add a "Notes for Editors" section, after making it clear that the press release has ended, with links to any references for research/statistics/reports etc. to which you have referred in the main body of the press release.

And be sure to include your contact details (name, company name, email address, telephone number).

178 Use short sentences

Using short sentences, with good grammar, makes a press release easy and quick for the reader to digest.

179 Do your due diligence

Ensure your facts and figures are well researched and resourced. Double and triple check your sources so you can be sure that everything is accurate. Get permission for using any photos and ensure that you credit the person appropriately. It is very important to get this right. See "Notes for Editors" in **177 Structure the press release**.

For example, the story I broke, "Insensitive language forces Boots signage change", was covered by another outlet which credited someone who shared the photo on X (formerly Twitter). Dynamically Disabled Life Coach and Abstract Artist Kekezza Reece wrote to the journalist asking him to credit appropriately and to provide payment! (You might not have to pay for any photo you have copied from social media but it is essential to ask permission and credit appropriately.)

180 Send links to images

Include a link to a Dropbox or WeTransfer folder with a selection of images from which the recipient can choose. You could also include the press release in this folder. Some email programs won't accept attachments and the recipient will only want to look at pictures if the press release has already grabbed their attention. Some journalists will not open what looks like a press release if there are attachments, thinking the press release is an attachment and every second counts!

CHAPTER 7 Sending out press releases

181 Include a variety of images

Often people just send portrait pictures. But you'll find that actually landscape are often more sought after because they are the perfect format for a paper layout and how we most often read online. They take up less space vertically and fit screens better, without having writing wrapped around them.

See **40** Have photos ready and consider professional photos

182 Check out local news publishing sites

You may find a local news outlet where you can publish your press releases for free, if they are relevant to your area. For example, I am a school governor and invited TV judge Rob Rinder to visit. We sent out a press release and uploaded it to *London Daily News*. Paid users can upload as many times as they like.

183 Sell your story to a news agency

This works well if you have a breaking news story but works for lifestyle and amusing stories too. It is particularly good if you have an accompanying picture. Journalists from Jam Press can work with you to write the story and negotiate a price with news publishers, or distribute it as a press release, so that you may appear in more than one outlet.

Kekezza Reece sold her story about Boots and the "Less-Abled" parking sign and photo (mentioned earlier) to Jam Press, which got placed in the *Daily Telegraph*, *Mirror* and *Daily Mail*.

Caters Media Group works in a similar way and, like Jam Press, operates worldwide.

184 Get on distribution lists

Sign up to organisations' press release lists. This will help you keep abreast of what is going on in your industry and may give you ideas to use in your own press release.

So, for example, a retail analyst may sign up to receive press releases from large retailers. When the retailer sends out press releases about their financial reports, the analyst can simultaneously provide relevant insightful commentary and send it to journalists.

This works particularly well if a press release is embargoed (delayed), as it gives you time to write something relevant. For example, an organisation may be announcing the launch of a new product or service for two days' time. But they send the press release early to give journalists time to plan covering that story. You must honour this embargo but you can still send a press release referencing it, also embargoed.

For example, in talking to Mark Morrell (also known as Mr Pothole), I got added to the Asphalt Industry Alliance's press release list and then wrote a press release using information from one of theirs with a quote from Mark. This got a variety of coverage online, radio and TV, such as *BBC Breakfast*, for both of us.

185 Collaborate

Work with other experts in your field in building your network. For example, I've written press releases including other money bloggers, consumer rights information, quoting cyber safety experts, etc. One of these got coverage in the *Financial Times* with "Money saving travel tips to lift the gloom of 'Blue Monday'" and another gave a money blogger her first TV appearance on *BBC Breakfast*.

If you have an angle, you can ask around for other experts to contribute and give your press release more clout.

You are seeking to pool your expertise and/or back each other up in commentary (or to give opposing views) on a story currently in the press. This will come from building relationships with people in network groups and finding out about others with your interests, for example in Lightbulb.

See **25** **Facebook Lightbulb group**.

CHAPTER 7 Sending out press releases

186 Promote products appropriately

It is acceptable to promote your products if something you provide is topical or you can find a good angle. If so, then pitch it as an idea in Lightbulb or send as a press release. If you have a great review from someone, you could use a sentence in the title. So, for example, if it's a National Day for Mental Health Awareness and you sell well-being products, write a press release about how certain products can help, putting yours as an example. But please remember, it should not be solely a pitch for your product. You need a hook.

See **86** Use Awareness Days/Weeks/Months to highlight your expertise.

187 "Out of office" responses

When you start sending your press releases, you may get lots of "Out of office" email responses which provide additional names, email addresses and telephone numbers. Add them to your list, saying "Thank you very much for being out" in your head, as you do so! Then email those people and add them to your list for next time.

If a journalist has moved on to another role then their auto-reply may contain contact information for the new person inheriting that beat. Be sure to take note and update your master list.

188 Realistic expectations

When you send your press releases, don't assume that the recipients will 'bite' every time!

Being consistent, by regularly landing in inboxes with useful/interesting information, is key. Over the years I've sent press releases and then got a response back to ask me to talk about something completely different. Build up being known for your expertise and they will come to you anyway but they need to keep seeing you.

HOW TO GET FREE PR FOR YOUR BUSINESS & BE PAID FOR IT

189 Be proactive with press releases

Do searches on anniversaries, for example the 50 year anniversary of an event related to your industry. If you specialise in SEO, it could be the anniversary of when the Internet started or the debut of the World Wide Web. That can help you to formulate the hook for a press release or pitch to a local outlet.

Make sure you are always answering the "So what?", "Why now?" and "Why you?" questions.

See **86** Use Awareness Days/Weeks/Months to highlight your expertise.

190 Be controversial in your press release

Ryanair's Michael O'Leary gets almost guaranteed press coverage for his unique and often controversial views but don't do a Ratner!

See **60** Be controversial in mainstream media, **130** Be controversial on air and **239** Be controversial on social media.

> Gerald Ratner was the CEO of Ratners, a chain of jewellery shops. In the 1990s he jokingly made a comment about the poor quality of some of the company's products. What followed nearly saw the company go bankrupt. It is still referred to as "Doing a Ratner", decades on!

191 Create a problem!

Then solve it! What have you got that solves a problem? For example, talk about the problem and carry out a survey on social media, demonstrating how your product(s) or service improves it.

Be careful of just selling in a press release, as no one will take the story if it is

CHAPTER 7 Sending out press releases

solely promotional. A press release that captures a journalist's interest needs to be more than simply a product release and must contain some additional attraction/story which persuades the reader to engage with it.

192 Try and break a record!

Daft as it may seem, take something that might just be achievable and ask the press to cover the record-breaking attempt! I thought about breaking the record for talking but in 2004 Lluis Colet set a Guinness World Record for making the longest speech ever. It came in at 48 hours. I don't think even I could do that, and if I could, that record was broken again, by the same man. In 2009 he spoke for 124 hours. Now, I know I could rant for a very, very long time but I don't think I could do it for more than 124 hours! He was French but press coverage of his record crossed the water to the UK.

There are, however, many records you could try to break and get media coverage because a record is a record, right? Even better if you can relate it to your work. For example, if you make T-shirts, how about attempting to beat the record for the most T-shirts put on in a minute (at the point of publishing it was 31!).

Practice, make an event, do it as a fundraiser, make sure you fulfil the criteria for officially breaking the record and invite the press.

It doesn't even matter if you fail really, as you can create a buzz on social media by, for example, putting out a video of the attempts.

193 Time when you send press releases out

Typically, emailing early in the day is considered the best time to pitch. Most newspaper editorial planning meetings happen before 10.00am. However, I have sent press releases after this time and they have been used on the radio later.

Certainly, when sending out a comment on a breaking piece of news, you want to get it out as quickly as possible.

See **203** Newsjack.

194 Set up Google Alerts for your keyword interests

Set up alerts for subjects in your area of expertise. For example, I have alerts set up for various consumer words, such as "Ombudsman" and "consumer rights". This will help you to keep track of breaking stories on which you can offer comment or write about.

195 Keep an eye out for relevant issues

For example, a number of my press releases have been about Alternative Dispute Resolution (ADR) providers. So, because I keep an eye on what the Civil Aviation Authority (CAA) does, I discovered that there was a CAA consultation about ADR.

However, because I am on the CAA press release list I questioned why I had not received notification. I discovered that it had failed to consult with stakeholders regarding proposed changes. I sent out a press release exposing the issue and got the CAA's deadline for responses extended. The story was covered in *This Is Money* and I got an all-important mention and hyperlink to my website.

196 Tipoffs

Some media outlets will pay you for a tipoff for a story. For example, a few years ago, before I was writing articles of my own, I tipped off the *Financial Times* about BA telling people to contact their insurance company when they couldn't fly, following a computer system outage. I got paid £250 for the tip. This kind of thing is good if you want to act very quickly or don't have the time to write a full press release. You should also get the credit and another "as seen in" entry.

CHAPTER 7 Sending out press releases

197 Make a direct pitch

Research the outlet in detail. What is it they are looking for? How can you fit their criteria? What problem can you solve? Then make a direct pitch to a journalist at the outlet.

See **18** Research the outlet and **255** Pitch to editors.

Usha Singh-Das bought a property at auction. She contacted the BBC *Homes Under the Hammer* show and the property development was filmed for the programme.

Keep the pitch short, at one to two paragraphs maximum. I recently had someone who had seen an article I had written in the *Metro* message me on LinkedIn. His pitch was so long it took two messages! He had written the article! No journalist wants the article written for them!

Have a strong angle, a solid story, offer photographs and say that more information is available.

198 Direct approach on the phone!

Although I prefer email, there is no reason why you can't use the phone, too! Pick up the phone and call the switchboard of the outlet in which you would like to appear. Ask to speak to a producer on the show. Be prepared, have all your credentials ready and the topics you would like to discuss and feel qualified to do so.

Have 3-5 key topics you would feel comfortable to talk about. So, for example, for me it would be complaining effectively, complaining in each different sector, money saving and customer service, and then go into more detail about any topic that piques an interest.

Having researched the programme thoroughly, you will be able to suggest how and why you would be a good fit. Remember, you are selling yourself here.

Don't phone when the show is being broadcast, if it's live, try to catch the production team on another day!

See **7** Contact your local radio station.

199 Predict something

Predict a trend.

For example, if you are a supplier of toys, predict the most likely top-selling products at Christmas. Or if you work in the wedding industry, making cakes, predict the most popular flavour or design for the season.

200 Facts, figures and statistics

News outlets LOVE this!

Undertake a fun and/or interesting survey and if it produces some great statistics send a press release. If you can hook this to something in the news, even better. For example, if there is a royal christening coming up, you could run a survey on how many people buy second hand, reuse, make a christening robe, etc.

Remember to try and stand out, produce interesting facts unlikely to be revealed by others.

201 Keep it short and sweet

There is no point overloading a journalist's inbox with lengthy rambling press releases, even if you think all of that text is oh-so-interesting.

So, train yourself to keep it short and sweet, one printed page of A4 at maximum. Doing this will compel you to hone your message and convey the vital elements in the most effective way.

202 Piggyback press releases

If an organisation has put out a press release in an area related to your expertise and you can work quickly, you can send out a comment with a link to their

CHAPTER 7 Sending out press releases

work. This can, in theory, get coverage for both organisations.

I have done this many times and my comments have often been included on a wider piece about a current affairs subject. For example, when a regulator, such as Ofcom or Ofgem introduces a new rule, I'll comment on it. A short comment is easy to copy and paste into an article.

You can use the comment in context on your website, see **206** **Put your press release on your website**.

203 Newsjack

Newsjacking is the term given to individuals or businesses promoting themselves by joining in the current news of the day.

After reading this book, you will be keeping an eye out for what is the news. This means that you will be able to 'newsjack' more easily. This might be putting your comments on the news with an Instagram post, a blog post or sending out a press release with expert comment.

I do this a lot. For example, I received a press release from the regulator Ofcom on complaints data and wrote up a press release with comment which was used by a journalist in *This is Money* "Most complained-about broadband, TV and phone firms revealed".

Even if the outlet doesn't use your comment, your expertise is regularly hitting the journalist's inbox.

See also **206** **Put your press release on your website**.

204 Plagiarism

Please don't plagiarise other people's work! If you are researching other outlets for your own pieces, ensure you credit the source and put quotation marks around anything you include. If something is appearing in the news, you can of course give your comment.

Be careful about using material that only appears in one outlet! I came across a blogger who had written an article regarding something in the news. I was on

BBC Breakfast talking about it. This had come from a press release that I had sent regarding changes to Ofcom regulations. This blogger had looked up my post (the press release in first person) and had taken information from it. Whilst the majority of it was in the public domain, she took a small chunk that I had received in response to a question to the Ofcom Press Office…!

I wouldn't ever look at her blog normally, as there is so little on it and hardly any original material, but it came to me via another email and the title raised suspicions. So, don't think people won't see because they wouldn't look at where you post!

I often quote motivational speaker Brad Burton, who says "You'll never be the market leader copying the market leader."

205 Press release distribution services

There are many outlets which for a fee will distribute your press releases. Before you start to build your list this may appeal. However! Use a site like Slashdot which lists companies which do this and provide a free trial. Most are not in the UK but some are and it's great if you want to communicate globally!

Only use one at a time, as many contacts will be doubled up but you should be able to get a few free trials!

206 Put your press release on your website

Once you have sent out your press release, publish it on your website in your blog/latest news. Post it on LinkedIn, make a free image in Canva and include it with your press release on Instagram. Consider creating a short TikTok video or Instagram reel, too, to cover the story.

You can put this in the first person, if necessary, if you were used as a quote in the press release.

One of the first and most successful press releases I sent out was back in 2016, titled "Looking a gift card in the mouth?" Two weeks after sending it I was recording for The One Show and the information I provided was used alongside my appearance. This gives you content for your blog/website and the video/radio link etc. and adds value, as well as showing your credibility.

207 Use Google News

Search Google and the "News" tab for ideas on how you can hook your news into something topical. Put in your possible headline and search to see what there has been in the papers and news websites over the last week or two.

See **194** Set up Google alerts for your keyword interests.

208 Don't send out if something big is in the news

If something big is breaking there is little point in sending a press release as it will just get lost. Hold onto it to send at a later time.

209 Don't plan to send out if big news is planned

On a similar note to **208** **Don't send out if something big in the news**, if you know that significant events are planned, such as royal weddings or funerals, then don't plan to send out a press release in the days before and after the event. It may be worth sending a related press release though.

See **203** **Newsjack**.

210 Get quotes

When writing your press release, try to include quotes from experts. These help bring the piece alive, show the expertise and may be used in a different article. For example, a journalist may be writing an article using various sources and take a quote from your press release to use.

See **203** Newsjack.

211 Measure pitch success rate

If you are using a mail marketing program, such as Mailchimp, Mailerlite or ActiveCampaign, measure how many emails were read, replied to and the success rate. You'll also be able to monitor which type of subject lines get opened, as well as which ones get a reply. You may need to tweak your PR plan as you go.

See **4** Read the book and make a plan!

CHAPTER 8

Boost your profile outside of traditional media

Public Relations is not just about TV, radio, newspapers and magazines. There is so much opportunity to raise your profile elsewhere, particularly on the Internet.

You want the public to think that you are so frequently featured on a wide variety of platforms that it's hard to miss you! This will ensure people know that you are good at what you do and that you can help them.

212 Be active on Facebook

In Facebook groups, get included in directories, network, give advice in—and offer to speak in—the groups. Many often have a day per week/month of live networking about what you can offer, which raises your profile, too. So, for example, The Delegate Wranglers on Facebook is for professional conference organisers and events industry suppliers.

For one hour a day, once a week, there is a *#Supplierhour* where you can pitch your product or service to event and conference organisers. Lightbulb has a three hour session every week for businesspeople to share what they do, which is always popular, particularly for podcasters looking for guests.

Diane Ivory of Forensic Minds posts regularly on the *#Supplierhour* but because she is also very active in the group, members often recommend her. She has gained lots of speaking and team building events, mainly for corporates, from this source.

So, undertake searches for networking and business groups. Also try Facebook groups in your niche markets, where you can offer help. I regularly speak in numerous groups and memberships about consumer rights and complaining effectively and customer service, complaint handling, exceeding expectations and complaint handling. This in turn means I reach more people and many of them will download the freebie so I have their email address.

213 Run a competition

This is a great way to get noticed. If you sell products, run a competition to win one. It helps spread the word if people are sharing your website and your details and you may get some sales along the way!

Be careful if you're running a competition on Facebook. If you break their rules, your page might be closed down. You could also be breaking the law.

Zaria Sleith, a Meta-Certified Community Manager and brand photography expert, advises that competitions on Facebook are allowed as long as no money changes hands. See "Facebook Pages, groups and events" for terms and conditions. You can do it for likes, votes, or a link to an entry form on your own website.

She warns "As long as the participants don't need to pay an 'entry fee' to take part, no licence is needed. To obtain gambling licences you need a physical premises and there are LOTS of restrictions and boxes to tick to get it from the local council!"

Raffles, tombolas and sweepstakes are all classed as lotteries. See the Gambling Commission's advice on "Types of lottery you can run without a licence".

214 Fill out your Facebook "About" information

When you post and make comments, whether in network, publicity or general interest groups, members will click on your name to find out more about you.

I can assure you that, as a journalist, I have been interested in something someone has said and looked them up only to find no information about them.

CHAPTER 8 Boost your profile outside of traditional media

I recently saw a call in Lightbulb for expert comment about saving money. A respondent spoke about refurbished technology and I thought he would be interesting to interview on *The Complaining Cow Consumer Show*. But I clicked on his name and found no contact details. So, I had no idea about his specific expertise and whether his work was related to his comment or not. You need to make yourself easy to find out about for journalists (and indeed customers) or they will be off on another route.

215 Put your freebie link on your cover photo on Facebook

You may feel that your friends and family won't want to see your work. But if they are friends they won't mind, as it doesn't make any difference to them?! Also in their feed your cover photo doesn't come up. But people new to you, whether journalists or through networking, will look at your home page. They will check your "About" (see **214 Fill out your Facebook "About" information**) but they will see your picture first.

Create an image in Canva (it's free). Select Facebook cover photo, upload an image and add the title of your freebie if you have one (a download to provide value and for you to gain the person's email address) or to join your FB group. The freebie will be something that visitors can get in return for providing you with their email address, so you can add them to your mailing list.

On my Facebook cover picture, for example, I have "Click here to find out more about The Complaining Cow and join my FB group". It's just added to my picture of lots of chocolate bars! When visitors click on the cover photo they can read a blurb about you and your work and links, such as your website, freebie, Facebook group, etc.

216 Start a YouTube channel

Set up a YouTube channel and film short videos demonstrating your expertise. Give tips, talk on a topical issue, as well as evergreen pieces that will hold interest at any time. These can be embedded in your website, giving more content, as well as showing the media that you are comfortable in front of a camera.

I have a YouTube channel on which I put a mixture of my media appearances and home-made videos, with advice on complaining effectively, topical issues and pieces of advice for businesses. It means that it's another outlet for visitors to find and I insert many of them into relevant blog posts, too.

217 Record or request footage

When you're on the television, record the appearance or ask for the footage, so you can put it onto your YouTube channel and/or embed on your website.

218 Ask your audience!

If you are looking for ideas, ask your audience what they would like to see. In your social media channels, ask questions around your work. What would be helpful to them, run a poll, what they think of a topical situation etc. The results can later be used in a press release.

219 Involve your MP!

My MP is Iain Duncan Smith (IDS). Several years ago I decided to go to an MP's surgery with him and record it (audio). At the time he was the Secretary of State for the DWP. I challenged him on such matters as the 'Bedroom Tax', ATOS and foodbanks. I went back a second time, too. I would have hoped to have made him consider his actions but I don't think I did. However, they were the first entries on my YouTube channel.

My premise is complaining effectively, so I took people's complaints to IDS. If you can find a link between your business and your MP, you could ask her/him for an interview, go to a surgery, ask about a specific policy and how it relates to something in your life. Your audience will like seeing you take action and engaging with your MP.

If you have a responsive MP, you can still take an issue affecting your customers, for instance. You can then use the story if they give you a quote about what they will be doing. Think of the times MPs take a constituent's story to the House of Commons.

CHAPTER 8 Boost your profile outside of traditional media

It could be your story being featured, if you have something appropriate.

220 Build relationships with big businesses

This can offer a number of opportunities. For example, when I started *The Complaining Cow* blog I embarked on a complaint about Tesco. Within a year I took them to court over something else and won. By that time there were a few posts about Tesco on the blog. A year later a new Group CEO, Dave Lewis, had been appointed. I wrote to him, congratulating him on the new role, and directing him to my blog!

Over the next few years, we built up a working relationship. This included writing a guest blog post for them and them writing one for my site, which all helped with improving reach. Dave mentioned me in one of his financial reports and I visited the offices where they test new products. I then interviewed Matt Davies, the Tesco UK CEO, and Dave together in an exclusive interview. I took questions from past, present and future customers. Tesco did the editing and put it on their website and YouTube channel. At the point of publishing it has had about 15,000 views. The page "Case Study: Tesco and a Consumer Champion" charts the court case, meetings, blogs posts and the interview.

So, if you provide a service or a way of challenging a business, get in touch with them. Something may develop and whatever way it goes, for example in working together, you may have a story that you can take to the press.

If you want to contact the boss of a company you can get the details from *ceoemail.com* or try the company's press office.

221 Contact bloggers

If you have a product, see if a blogger will review it? Some will charge for this service but others will provide a review in return for the product. The UK Money Bloggers community is a good place to start. They will publicise your post and your product or service will reach a new audience.

222 Podcasts

Join some Facebook groups where podcast presenters and people who want to be on podcasts meet. Although most won't have huge audiences, it gives you practice, experience of a new audience and you can put links on your website for editors and reporters to assess your expertise and delivery.

Podcast Connection and Podcast Guest Collaboration are two International ones. Based in the UK a newer player on the block started Business GROWTH Opportunities Through GUEST Appearances. This started in response to many people leaving a large group which appeared to be full of people charging guests to be on a podcast.

Don't pay to be on a podcast, as you can reach more people by using the money on advertising and marketing! One was even charging for her first episode so, yes, with an audience of zero!

Julia Starzyk, a Quantity Surveyor and Project Manager, founder of Star Projects, answered a request to be a guest on the podcast *Bust and Beyond*. She and the host had a pre-podcast chat and it became apparent that the host's background was similar. He invited her to deliver a guest presentation for his membership. This then led to more follows and sales.

223 Podmatch

Podmatch is an online service which matches up podcasters and guests.

This website has a limited free subscription. It allows you to put in 10 key areas that you can talk about and will match you up with three possible podcasts per day or more if you upgrade. The majority of the podcasts are from the US but there are some from the UK.

224 MatchMaker.fm

Covering the world, *MatchMaker.fm* connects podcasters with guests. Set up a profile as a guest, provide a picture, a headline and some notes about yourself and podcasters can contact you. You can also search podcasts and offer to be a guest.

The free version lets you have 10 conversations a month. The paid for version offers priority search listing, upload of a video pitch and being able to post to the community to ask for help.

225 Listen to podcasts

If there are a couple of podcasts that you really want to get onto, listen to a couple of episodes first. This will give you an idea of the kinds of questions they ask their guests. And then assess whether what you do fits their podcast before pitching to go on it.

226 Prepare for a podcast as you would any other interview

Usually, you'll have longer on a podcast than other types of interview. You therefore have more of a chance to get across what you would like to say. So, you can have lots of written notes as reminders and even read some sections because most are recorded with sound only!

See also **CHAPTER 2 Prepare for your coverage**.

227 Set up your own podcast

This is something I would have started a few years ago, if I had had the time.

If you're at the beginning of your journey in building your PR, consider setting up a podcast. Find your niche and just talk about it! Get guests, too. Don't be disheartened when you have no audience to begin with, as it's very slow to take off unless you already have a big following.

You have to build your audience, which will grow if you are consistent. And, of course, push it out yourself on social media. As your audience grows, they will go back and listen to old episodes. If you have a website and/or a blog, embed the podcast in your site.

If you have recording equipment, you can actually set up your own podcast for free. If not, you can usually get what's needed for under £100. But I record for radio just using my laptop and built-in microphone!

Dr Marianne Trent's *The Aspiring Psychologist* podcast had been running for ten months when she was contacted by a producer from *Channel 5* asking if she would be interested in auditioning for a new series. Within a week she had been cast for the four-part series *Inheritance Wars: Who gets the cash?*

228 Reach out to influencers

The key to getting good coverage from influencers is to ensure that you target well.

In 2020 Rachael Lainé bought Le Tricoteur, a traditional Guernsey knitwear company which had never undertaken any social media.

In 2023 she gifted a jumper to Erica Kim, an Instagram influencer. She personally follows Erica as she admires her classic pared-back style with no make-up and no-fuss photos. Rachael recommends reaching out to those you follow for a reason and asking before sending anything. Erica, for example, will only accept gifts she knows she will wear, so as to avoid waste.

In Rachael's case, Erica still posts and Rachael gets more followers each time.

229 Join influencer marketing Facebook groups

Most influencers will charge for promoting your product. However some just starting out, or with smaller followings, will accept being gifted the product.

Look at the Facebook group Influencer/Blogger Assignments & Opportunities. In that group you can make offers to see if any influencers would be interested.

CHAPTER 8 Boost your profile outside of traditional media

230 Start a Facebook group full of your ideal clients

Now this can be a lot of time and effort. And at some point you can sell to the people in there, but the group is where you can do 'lives' and provide lots of tips and advice to help members and show yourself as the expert. But, it's somewhere you can grow your audience, ask questions and give/gain support. Again, giving away things for free but you will be able to reap the rewards.

For example, Georgina Nestor used to run a free group and her advice was superb.

See **63 Get reviews from customers**. She gave this advice in a group and I copied and pasted it to keep and use! Many, many months later I went back to her to ask if I could use it for this book. She now has a page in this book!

231 Do your own videos

This may seem daunting, but when you are starting out it shows researchers and producers that you are comfortable on camera. Make short clips with tips on your area of expertise for YouTube, Instagram, Facebook or TikTok. Repurpose material on social media and start your own channels, giving advice.

Set up a YouTube channel and film short videos demonstrating your expertise. Give tips, talk on a topical issue, as well as evergreen pieces that will hold interest at any time.

These can be embedded on your website, giving more content, as well as showing the media that you are comfortable in front of a camera.

I have a YouTube channel on which I put a mixture of my media appearances and home-made videos, with advice on complaining effectively, topical issues and pieces of advice for businesses. It means that it's another outlet when people search Google and I insert many of them into relevant blog posts, too.

In addition to my YouTube channel, I also do videos for my TikTok and Instagram accounts. Videos giving advice do well.

Jenny Leggott was very wary of doing videos. She says:

"I was really scared of being filmed. So scared I nearly backed out. But it was Helen who persuaded me to give it a go. She was very direct about it and showed me outtakes of her videos so I could see it didn't have to be perfect first time. I wrote my speech word for word and practised in front of a mirror until I was happy it wouldn't be a disaster".

After you have gone through that much preparation and put out a few videos you will be quicker and need less preparation.

Tom Stanhope, a professional video producer, has these tips for making your own videos:

1. **Get to Know Your Audience:** Think of your viewers as friends you haven't met yet. What do they like? What gets them excited? The better you understand them, the more engaging your videos will be!

2. **Focus on Quality and Relevance:** Keep your videos sharp and clear, both in picture and sound. And remember, content is king! Make sure what you're sharing is something your audience will find useful or fun.

3. **Tell a Story That Sticks:** Everyone loves a good story, right? Make sure your video has a clear and captivating storyline. Whether it's a quick laugh, a heartwarming moment, or a mind-blowing fact, keep it interesting!

4. **Give a Little Nudge:** Don't be shy to tell your viewers what to do next. A friendly call to action, like inviting them to visit your website or follow your socials, can go a long way.

5. **Engage and Interact:** Remember, video isn't just a one-way street. Encourage viewer interaction by asking questions, inviting comments, or even running polls. This not only boosts engagement but also helps you learn more about your audience's preferences and opinions. Plus, it's a fun way to make your viewers feel like they're part of the journey.

Or do videos for TikTok where it is easier to reach more people and go viral.

See **144** Agent and **269** **Use the content for a blog post**.

CHAPTER 8 Boost your profile outside of traditional media

232 Join Grow Your Business with Video group on Facebook

Tom Stanhope runs a free Grow Your Business with Video group on Facebook. Tom regularly goes live in the group and provides tips and answers questions etc.

233 Do videos for other people

If you are comfortable producing and appearing in videos, make them for other people. For example, I started doing storytelling and read from books as well as improvising for my storytelling channel. This meant that people for whom I did storytelling shared the videos. In the description beneath each video, I link to my website, products & services and social media. On the channel I link to everything of mine. I also then started charging for this service.

234 Collect emails

When people see you in the media, they may look you up and find your website. Ensure you have an email address collection form on your home page so you can keep them informed and at some point sell to them. Ensure you are GDPR compliant.

235 Social media

Posts that go viral can get you coverage on social media, shared to potential new customers, get picked up by the mainstream media and increase your following. Never miss an opportunity to highlight something funny or absurd that happens in your life!

236 Go live

Although not strictly media or speaking on stage, going 'live' on Facebook or X (formerly Twitter) is a good way for your followers on social media to get to know you and ask questions. This will build your confidence, provide more material that you can repurpose and will increase your audience.

237 If you don't ask, you don't get

For my first book *How to Complain: The Essential Consumer Guide for Getting Refunds, Redress and Results!* I asked consumer journalist Paul Lewis for a review, which now features on the back of the book. I subsequently asked him for an interview on his personal complaining habit for my blog.

When it came to my second book, *101 Habits of an Effective Complainer*, I secured a foreword from Paul Lewis and reviews from TV journalist, Matt Allwright, and TV Judge Robert Rinder.

Some months later I obtained an interview with Matt on his personal complaining habits and a couple of years later an interview on my radio show. I asked for even more from Rob Rinder! I requested an interview with him about his career, what his plans were and his personal complaining habits. He kindly agreed. I recorded an interview over Zoom and split it into 3 different blog posts and various short clips. This meant that viewers could watch the whole interview and that I could share different parts of it on social media. There is no rule that says you can only use your PR once! In fact, you should always find ways of using it more than once!

In the interview Rob also made some complimentary comments about the work I do and so that is now a videoed testimonial, too. Testimonials from those with a high profile bring even more credibility.

Think about whom you could approach for an interview. Who in your area of work is in the public eye? Can you piggy-back on the PR work of others in your field?

I happened to mention to Rob that I was doing another book and it was near the proof stage and even though it's not consumer or legal stuff, he offered to do a review of this one. This probably says more about him being a nice chap than anything else but it does show what comes from a cheeky request in the first place and that you probably should just ask!

For this book I also asked Jeremy Vine to do the foreword and Eddie Nestor to do a review.

238 Practice on social media posts

Facebook and LinkedIn are especially good for getting information to a business audience. You can write posts and repeat them to see what engagement you get and what topics resonate with the audience. Talk about relationships, hobbies, business and health, etc. Journalists don't tend to hang out there looking at posts unfortunately. But it will help you in getting confidence in writing, building a network and raising your profile. Journalists love to read about—and cover—an individual's business journey and anything out of the ordinary.

Experts such as Helen Tudor and Lea Turner help businesses get leads on LinkedIn and it's worth following them and checking out their posts and free challenges for tips on raising your profile.

Lisa Johnson is a business strategist who runs a variety of free challenges, including one on visibility which will help you raise your social media game.

239 Be controversial on social media

This is great for getting coverage! If you are going to polarise opinions, not only will you get more supporters and followers of your work/social media but the people who disagree will engage in posts and boost your reach!

Maddy Alexander-Grout tried an experiment. In 2022 she posted a picture of herself wearing a low cut top to see what reaction she would get on what is a professional networking platform. The picture went with a work-related post. She was disgusted to be inundated with sleazy messages. This story got picked up by the *Daily Mail*, where commenting was turned off: "Woman who posted a LinkedIn photo showing 'a little bit of cleavage' as an experiment says she faced 'sleazy comments' and 150 connection requests from men, as well as calls to do more to protect women."

See **60** Be controversial in mainstream media, **130** Be controversial on air, and **190** Be controversial in your press release.

240 Try a Q and A or free webinar

Whip up some interest with your customers and audience in your social media channels and newsletters. This could be a set time on X (formerly Twitter) with a hashtag for say an hour where you will answer questions on a particular topic. Or set up a free (or for a small charge!) webinar where you impart lots of your expertise and answer questions.

This helps with your exposure as well as giving you practice. You can also record the webinar (ensure you have consent from all participants to do so) and edit into bitesize videos for your website and on your social media that you can put out over time to keep momentum going.

Don't forget to ask any attendees for a review too!

James Bore, a Chartered Security Professional from Bores Group ran a free online business continuity scenario for a group of 40 attendees. The attendees were assigned roles during a fictional cyber security incident, from defending the company to being part of the attacking group, and ran through the stages of the scenario discussing the actions they would take and finding out the results. As a direct result, several attendees booked in-person business continuity and crisis management workshops for their own businesses, and after the recording was released (with permission of the attendees) more followed.

241 Comment

Spot a relevant news story on which you have a perspective and share it on social media, together with your opinion. If it's in the news that penguins are to join the Olympics then retweet the story with reasons why this would not be a good idea. Ask for the opinion of others, showing that you are connected to the topic and are passionate about it.

Some journalists look for stories and comments on X (formerly Twitter). So, if there is something trending on X and you have an opinion that shows you as an expert on the topic then make a comment. Blog about it and share. You never know who might pick it up. Writing about it on a blog on your website also means that as you build this you will be demonstrating authority when journalists look you up.

Add this to your social media strategy to do regularly as a weekly activity.

242 Share the opportunities

When you see opportunities on *#JournoRequest* or similar and think they would be good for someone in one of your networks, share them. This keeps your name up there in groups as a helpful person so that journalists will watch you, as well as getting others to possibly reciprocate.

243 Email signature

In your email use a standard 'signature' with links to your website and social media. Link to any particular media coverage, too. It all helps to raise the profile as email recipients look at your links.

My email has links to my website, all my social media and showreel.

244 Charities

Get involved with a charity for a 'win-win'. Feel good stories always go down well, particularly for local print and radio outlets. Choose a cause which is meaningful to you and that you would genuinely like to support. Don't fake charity work! Support and promote them and offer comment for their press releases, if appropriate.

245 Speaking at small events

If you lack the confidence, start small. Go to networking events where members can give presentations. For example, 4Networking is great for this. It has online and in-person events. For a membership fee plus £6 you can attend a meeting and network. But you can also attend one or two for free, to see if it's for you.

At these meetings you get to pitch you and your business for 40 seconds. 4Sight is another option, not a pitch but 20 minutes of giving some learning that can help business people in their work.

For example, I've done "20 ways to get free PR", the title of which is self-explanatory!

Another one I do is a Joyce Grenfell-style tale where I bring members of the group into the story and afterwards provide an interactive lesson in business.

But you don't have to be this creative. Others have held audiences with stories of their lives, overcoming hurdles, tips for all areas of business, with PowerPoint and without. You can invite people who have never been to a meeting to come, too, if you want some moral support!

When you are speaking, tell stories with which your audience can identify. For example, there are often statistics and reports on long waiting times in call centres.

In discussing such issues, it is always more interesting for people to hear anecdotes of how people have been affected and what you can do about it, rather than just producing a set of data.

246 Speaking at larger events

This subject would really need another book in itself to cover fully. The planning, introducing, content, getting on stage, getting over the nerves, how to present well, etc. There are already a number of resources out there to help. But the key points are:

1. Keep a note of invitations you get to events and ask if you can speak at the next one.
2. Provide a biography and relevant links when contacting the event organiser and write your introduction if you get the booking.

3. Tell stories.

4. Say what you are going to say, say it and then sum up.

5. Keep PowerPoint slides down to the minimum!

6. Your audience will want to be entertained, so bring in humour, too, if you can.

7. Follow the tips elsewhere in this book about preparation, feedback and improving confidence, if necessary.

247 Sign up to speaking agencies

For most agencies you will need to apply and provide footage and details of your experience. However, there are some where you can sign up yourself. These include Speakerhub, Speakernet and International Women's Day.

248 Plan your presentation effectively

In my previous life working in children's services I put together a number of presentations and found it always rather long-winded! I would just write everything out and try to remember it all.

I recommend Penny Haslam's book *Make Yourself a Little Bit Famous*. I bought this a few years ago and used her 'Affinity Method' to write my keynote. Genius. It was brilliant, completely new to me. It really focusses you onto the key points and structure AND, most importantly, the way you plan it out really helps in making you remember, without having to read anything.

249 Offer/respond to guest blog posts

Some outlets/bloggers will charge for this, if they see it is as advertisement, but many won't. You could do reciprocal posts. In your guest post on another site, provide value and insight into a topic and let the links to your information, such as your website and social media, do the advertising for you. This will help you reach a new audience, as the host will share the posts. The backlinks to your website help your SEO and drive traffic to your site. Other bloggers guest-writing for your site will do the same.

250 Offer a discount

Make writing a guest post for a blogger or an article for a paper more appealing by offering a discount on one of your products or services.

Years ago, when I was featured for an article "I'm proof it pays to complain, says woman who sued Tesco and WON" in *The Daily Express*, I offered signed copies of my book, not even at a discount, and sold many of them as a result! So, if you are used as a case study, try to offer a free product, as it looks good for the outlet, too.

I offer a 15% discount code for listeners of *The Complaining Cow Consumer Show*. Go listen if you want one!

See **10** Present local/community radio.

251 Celebrate other people's successes

Sometimes you can feel other people are getting lots of PR and you aren't, but don't get disheartened. It often comes in peaks and troughs and you have to keep putting yourself out there by following the tips in this book!

When experts or journalists share articles in groups, react and comment so people see you being positive. For example complimenting the journalist or the subject of a case study. (Be genuine, read the article first and refer to something that resonated, or was interesting etc.) Don't point out anything that could have been added or different. This could be taken as disrespectful to the journalist or case studies, detracting from the article.

Be aware that journalists have word counts or the editor could have cut the

CHAPTER 8 Boost your profile outside of traditional media

piece. If you are constantly trying to 'add value' to already published pieces you risk antagonising journalists rather than them thinking they should have included you/your words, even if that wasn't your intention. Imagine if everyone added something in a social media thread! Be respectful. You can always pitch an alternative view separately.

See **270** Try not to correct other experts!

252 Google listing

This is very easy to do, yet so few small businesses do it. Add your business as a Google listing. It's free and will come up in searches, showing a nice big entry with pictures. You will also be able to see, from the analytics provided by Google, the impact of this listing.

Go to *https://www.google.com/intl/en_uk/business/* to set it up. The prompts will take you through each stage in filling out the necessary information.

253 Awards

Winning an award can give you a lot of personal satisfaction, as well as add credibility to your work. There are, however, issues to consider when entering yourself/your business for an award or if you receive notification that you have won an award.

Be discerning when choosing which awards to enter. There are many awards now that charge for entries and have costly marketing packages.

However, consumers are beginning to get wise to pay-to-play awards and are losing faith in 'award winning' products and businesses, so choose wisely. But if you get shortlisted or win, you may at least have a story for your local paper. See "Corporate awards: Buyer beware!" on The Complaining Cow website for more discussion of this topic.

(254) Blog/website

Obviously, writing a blog is a fundamental part of my work and that means the media can find me through this. So, consider writing a blog for your website, too. Search engines like changing, regularly-updated and new content. So, it stands to reason that the more you have on a website, the more frequently you'll come up in search results, as long as you are writing high quality information and are good with other SEO elements!

Make sure that you shout about your media appearances on the blog/website too.

See also (67) **Work on your SEO,** (206) **Put your press release on your website,** (241) **Comment** and (249) **Offer/respond to guest blog posts.**

CHAPTER 9

Write yourself and get your name out there

As a blogger I obviously quite enjoy writing, which includes giving lots of expert quotes and opinion to media outlets.

In 2018 I started to pitch written articles to newspapers. The first was for the Financial Times which was quite a big hit to start off with! I helped the paper's consumer editor with resolving a case regarding his car hire. I then pitched an article around car hire, "Avoid a holiday hire car nightmare" about how he could have avoided the issue, how readers could protect themselves and how to complain if there was a problem. I'd already built up my credibility with the commissioning editor, as she had read my co-authored reports *Ombudsman Omnishambles* and *More Ombudsman Omnishambles* and I had appeared on her podcast.

I then started to pitch elsewhere. Over the last couple of years I have done this more often and it has become a main part of my business. Eventually I wrote a 'consumer champion' column for *This Is Money* and, of course, this helped book sales, raised my profile, as well as being paid for it.

Columns can help your PR because your name is there and you're sharing it, as are others. I tried for a number of years to get a consumer advice column. This was very difficult to do, as it would appear that once people have got them they don't move on! I also sought to do something a little different. I wanted to empower people and show how they could resolve a problem for themselves, rather than doing all the work for them.

To get a column you would normally have to show a considerable track record in journalism and demonstrate your subject expertise. If you have these already, think about outlets to which you can pitch. This does not have to be a big outlet. For example, you could write a column answering reader's problems about interior design for a specialist magazine. There will always be a niche outlet for your specific expertise.

Some publications may suggest you do this for free. It's worth considering if you don't have any experience yet. But when a national newspaper outlet asked me to do it for nothing, I said "no"! A few months later I was writing the column for *This Is Money*, reaching a far larger audience. But it depends where on your journey you are. Unfortunately, the column started just as lockdown was happening and so it never really took off and articles weren't placed regularly enough to gain momentum, so I moved onto other things.

255 Pitch to editors

Research publications and other outlets in which you would like to appear. Approach the relevant editor. Use the techniques outlined above for finding their email addresses. Give them different angles on your expertise, what you can write about and say you're open to suggestions, too.

Many publications are happy to receive pitches for opinion pieces told from your perspective. For example, use something from your personal life about which you have formed a strong opinion. Perhaps you had a traumatic experience on social media which has shaped your views of how social media should be regulated? If it is something that would polarise views, such as providing opinion on benefit pay out levels, then that is even more appealing to commissioners. (The advice about not reading comments below an article (known as below the line) is even more important if you write a divisive piece such as this!)

See **60** **Be controversial in mainstream media**.

For most outlets these commissions will mean a payment for your article but also get your name out there, as well as another item that you can add to your media coverage list. It also lets the outlet and others know that you can give expert comments.

Maddy Alexander-Grout, founder of the Mad About Money app, has appeared in *The Sun* a number of times with her money-saving tips. She now writes for them and gets paid, as well as having links to her business in the articles.

CHAPTER 9 Write yourself and get your name out there

256 Journo Resources

Journo Resources is a website that provides a mass of information on journalism, including free guides and advice. For example, they have journalists giving lots of "How to…"s. Their newsletter lists details of jobs in journalism, including freelance roles. You can receive limited access to newsletters for free. There is also a page of links to numerous specialist and some major outlets, covering a wide range of topics that take pitches. Whatever your expertise, check out the list and see if you can pitch an article that uses your knowledge.

257 Write at Home

Write at Home is similar to the above. This service provides a newsletter with journalist and writer positions available. It comes out twice weekly and offers a paid option, with access to past issues. There is a free trial month for receiving the email once a week.

258 Journo Resources Substack

This is a weekly free newsletter that lists various journalist jobs, including freelance positions. It also contains links to US call outs for pitches.

259 Freelance Writing Jobs

Sian Meades-Williams runs Freelance Writing Jobs and sends out emails every week which provide links to people and businesses looking for writers. She brings together call outs from commissioners on X (formerly Twitter). This could be for single pitches, freelance roles or full-time journalist positions. She covers absolutely any outlet, ranging from niche publications to the big nationals and glossies. So, you might find an opportunity to pitch an article that you can write and get paid for. This will show your knowledge and get you into the area of writing, if this appeals.

260 Use your successes to get more work

When you get a piece commissioned, don't forget to mention it when you pitch to others. For example, if you get a piece published in *Tesco* magazine, use it as a reference when pitching to *Sainsbury's Magazine*! It will be easier to get work the more you build up your portfolio and showcase it.

261 Get free expert help with pitching your writing

Punteha van Terheyden is a journalist, editor, ghost editor and is really rather brilliant and generous with her time. She runs the free Facebook group Succeed in Freelance Journalism in which she gives masses of tips, answers questions and even gives feedback on your pitches. If you have any thoughts about pitching to editors and writing articles yourself, then definitely join this group.

Punteha has generously offered readers of this book a 10% discount across her shop using the code HTCC10. This can be redeemed against her publications and mentoring sessions. I have two of the publications and they are really easy to read and follow!

CHAPTER 10

Performing at your best so you are asked back!

OK, so this may sound like the hardest thing, but it isn't! Remember, it is you who got yourself to this point and it's now time to go 'on stage'.

If you prepare well by following all the tips in **CHAPTER 2 Prepare for your coverage**, you will feel more confident going into the studio/location. If you have that confidence, you will perform better. Some people advise doing power poses before entering. (This supposedly puts you in a strong mind-set but don't get caught on camera...)

Many times I have come out of a live appearance and thought that it went too quickly and I didn't get across all that I wanted to say! This is particularly true for some outlets where they spend so much time discussing my personal branding, rather than getting on with the relevant issue!

262 Have water ready

Use room temperature water, as iced water can cause your throat to close up. You want water there to help you if you dry up through nerves or if you have spoken for a long time! Drink water before going on air.

263 Research the topic you're going to talk about

If you get asked to comment on the radio or TV about a current story in the news, ask for a copy of the material to be broadcast. Sometimes it may be an embargoed press release, so you can get early sight or they may have picked up a story online.

264 Be natural

If, like me, you talk a lot with your hands, use your hands. As soon as you try to not do something—or do something that you don't usually do—it will not come across well. You want people to identify with the 'real' you, not a 'fake' you.

Jenny Leggott says "The best advice I was given was to treat it as just another day in the office. Yes I can practice my words, take deep breaths and sips of water, but the idea that 'it's no big deal', it'll be over in X minutes, is how I managed to overcome pretty debilitating fears."

265 Buy time if necessary

If you need thinking time, repeat the question back. For example "Hmmm, would I say xyz, yes I think so, because..." shows that you are thinking in a measured way and communicating conversationally, ensuring a natural flow.

266 Don't worry if you think you went off course

If you feel you lost track and you want another stab at answering the question, say at the end "Did that answer your question?" This covers you, so that if the interviewer didn't get what they wanted, they can ask it again in a different way. I've done it! I do waffle sometimes but it has only happened a couple of times.

CHAPTER 10 Performing at your best so you are asked back!

You will find from experience that the interviewer rarely needs to ask again.

267 Ask for feedback

Don't labour this point but do ask the producer/director if they felt it went well and if they got everything they needed. In reality, no-one ever says how you could have improved, but it can give you a little confidence boost as you leave!

268 Be nice!

If people come round to your home to film or take photos or interview you, offer them a cup of tea or coffee, with biscuits! Most importantly, that's just polite! But you do want to show that you are good to work with, too!

269 Use the content for a blog post

Many times I've been asked to present about a topical subject on TV or radio about which I haven't already written. I then write a blog post about it and if it's TV and I've recorded it, that video gets embedded too. This means extra content for your website and another link for your media coverage page.

For example All you need to know about secondary tickets and touts which has a section of one of my appearances on *Channel 5 News* and also a clip from giving the information on Instagram. Adding information in various formats and platforms assists people who like a variety of ways to consume their information and helps your SEO.

See **231** **Do your own videos**.

270 Try not to correct other experts!

I'm probably not alone in struggling with this one! Once you start to do a lot of media, you may notice more often how others are getting facts wrong. It may be very tempting to contact a programme that you appear on or on social media. Try and just shout at the telly. For example, I often hear 'experts' telling people they can go to an Ombudsman where there isn't one for that sector.

I bet vets were shouting at the television when a so-called expert appeared on a magazine programme recently, telling people they could feed their dogs fruit and vegetables but didn't warn against giving them grapes and raisins, which can kill!

But I bet it annoyed Joe Nutkins even more. She says:

"I have seen programmes that have involved dogs and the info being given might be about my breed, Norwich Terrier, which causes me to have a shout at the TV as they are often confused with Norfolk Terriers or when Yorkshire Terriers are called the smallest of the Terrier Breed Group when they are actually a Toy Breed!"

After the event it is unlikely that a programme will put out anything about an item. So it will look like sour grapes.

See **154 Ignore the trolls on online articles, 155 Ignore the trolls on social media too**.

So, if you are going to 'correct' someone online, make sure that (a) your information is right! And (b) do it privately, otherwise you will look like a troll.

If you can't DM but you do want to give the right advice, that's all you can do.

But even then it doesn't always work. When I privately told a consumer journalist that her understanding of how an ombudsman works was misguided and a common misconception (and this was basic, nothing to do with the more complicated reports!), she said she had been in consumer affairs for over 20 years. So, I left it at that. There was no way she was going to grasp the complexities of an in-depth report if she couldn't even get the basics right!

271 Admit when you are wrong!

This is another area that can be difficult but important to understand. No-one is right all the time. So, if you admit and apologise when you get it wrong then it adds to your credibility and viewers/listeners will respect what you say.

For example, I once said that the UK national emergency text alert test didn't work on my phone. Someone said there was an issue with at least one of the providers. I posted that there wasn't and it was my phone. I was wrong, I quickly acknowledged and apologised on the Facebook post where I had said it.

I've seen people correct others on advice given and it not be acknowledged. Whilst I would advise you don't do this (see **270 Try not to correct other experts!**) it can make you look silly and rude if you have given the wrong advice and someone more knowledgeable than you has given the correct information. Say "Thank you" if you do your research and find they are right. I won't be alone in having more respect for the person who admits they are wrong.

272 Don't worry if the programme is running late!

Because, quite simply, they often are! Various reasons, schedules run over, last-minute changes etc. so if you're waiting down the line and wondering why they haven't come to you yet, don't worry, they will do.

273 Surround yourself with people whom you trust

Although you can be the leader in your field, we can't all know everything all the time. There will always be people who have more knowledge and experience in certain areas of your work than you do. And you certainly don't want to risk being wrong when it could be avoided!

For example, I have two lawyers, and two people who work in consumer rights to whom I always go to get clarity on anything about which I am not sure. Plus I have a positive connection with *Which?* I also have a fantastic friend and mentor. The result is a professional network where my work is valued and respected.

Don't worry if you do not have these cheerleaders or advisors around you. As your business develops, you will network more, do more media and encounter the people with whom you can work.

274 Milk it

Don't be scared of blowing your own trumpet! I've seen people do nothing with the media after their appearance. Sometimes they say that if they post on social media they think their friends and family won't be interested. If that's the case then they can scroll on by! Raising your profile isn't just about getting the media coverage, it's about putting it to use wherever you can and as often as you like!

The example from Susan in **146 Follow up appearances on social media** shows what can be achieved if you make the most of the opportunity to shout about your business.

275 Get a showreel made

When you have a substantial amount of media work behind you, consider making a showreel. You can do your own for free if you just want to get something out there. But at some point when you have a lot then you might want to get a professional one done.

My first showreel, made many years ago, was mostly radio but it was a start! The second showreel from a couple of years later was much better. I believe it is sensible to keep your showreel up to date, so more recently I created another showreel which included other outlets to show a range of coverage. The most difficult aspect, by that time was choosing what to put in and leave out!

However good your editing skills, a professional is going to be able to advise and show you at your best. In my experience, they will also take out your subjectivity when choosing clips! I have had many compliments from industry experts about my showreel, created by Tom Stanhope.

CHAPTER 10 Performing at your best so you are asked back!

See **144** **Agents**.

Don't use images from print. See **149** **Put up your coverage on your website**. You can use online work and your own photos. Repeating images or clips will look like you don't have enough material. Media folk don't watch to the end of showreels anyway! So it's fine to keep it short, a couple of minutes at maximum. A really good piece of feedback I was given by a programme editor on my most recent showreel was my voice should come first. I have since looked at other showreels and seen that many include introductions by other people. So, my video editor and I will think about it being "me first!"

Yes, it may seem unnatural to ask others to "Look at me!" But you have to get past that mindset to ensure you can push your PR as far as possible.

CHAPTER 11

Be true to yourself

"Be yourself; everyone else is already taken" said Oscar Wilde in one of his famous quotes. All PR for you is about YOU, so as soon as you start doing or saying things differently you will slip up.

Instead, simply stay true to your principles.

Another inspirational quote comes from the monk and poet, John Lydgate, who said "You can please some of the people all of the time, you can please all of the people some of the time, but you can't please all of the people all of the time."

---

276 Don't be afraid to say "no"

It's often very tempting to say "yes" to all possible appearances that you may be offered, particularly when you've been doing it for a few years and it's paid!

However, there may well be situations when it would not be in your best interests to say "yes". For example, I was asked to appear in a segment on mortgages. That is not in my area of expertise, so I turned it down. When I watched the mortgage expert's appearance I was extremely pleased that it had not been me! I'm not sure why I was even asked, as it is a technically complex area!

On another occasion I was invited to talk about sibling rivalry during one of the many times William and Harry Windsor were in the news! Again, I turned this down. Because, although I have opinions about most things, my area of expertise is already quite broad and this wouldn't be a topic with which I would want to be associated.

See **54** **Avoid a conflict of interest** and **277** **Keep your integrity**.

277 Keep your integrity

Long before I first appeared on BBC's The One Show, I was asked to be on the same programme in a segment about social media. They needed one person to argue the case for complaining on X (formerly Twitter) and Facebook. I believe that using social media does have its place but actually it is very limited. It is useful for speeding up the resolution of complaints, calling for help from major brands or for simple queries.

Otherwise, you will at some point have to take the issue offline.

The team wanted me to be more positive! I could not argue the case, particularly when this was several years ago and not so many companies were on X. So, as much as I wanted to be on the biggest magazine programme on TV, I turned it down. I could not contradict what I had already said on my own blog.

See **54** **Avoid a conflict of interest** and **276** **Don't be afraid to say "no"**.

278 Contact me!

If you think you might have a story in which I might be interested, see my commissions and contact me through my website.

See **20** **Email the journalist** and **21** **Research journalists and think about whether to typecast them**.

279 Keep on keeping on

As you have seen, building up your PR bit by bit and seizing all possible opportunities will, in turn, lead to more chances for media exposure of your product or service. You need to keep going, to continue build momentum and position yourself as the 'go to' expert for your specialist area. And by doing this you can benefit from the PR exposure you want for your products or services.

280 Keep it fun

There you have it!

I have used nearly all the tips (I've not attempted to break a record!) above and hope that what I have learnt over the last few years will help you along the way on your PR journey.

The most important thing to remember is to enjoy it. PR should be fun. Doing it yourself instead of employing a PR expert is a lot of work that cannot be underestimated.

Few people get more than one piece of PR with only luck. It is up to you to decide whether it is worth the time and effort to build up your PR yourself or to employ someone else to do it, instead.

Good luck—and enjoy!

Glossary

When you start working with the media you will sometimes read and hear terms that you haven't come across before or get confused by their different meaning in this context. Here's the low down.

Anecdote

Often people in the media will ask for these. They are looking for a short, often amusing story. But it should only be a few lines.

Aston

Title that appears on the television screen, with your name and description.

Appearance Fee

Quite simply, a fee for appearing on the TV or radio.

Beat

A journalist will sometimes talk about their particular beat. This will be their area of specialism, such as consumer, sport, politics or foreign affairs, for example.

Below the line

Comments written by the public beneath online articles.

Booker

Rarely used now, but this will be someone booking you onto the TV programme or radio show. The person doing this now will more likely be the **Researcher** (see below).

Byline
The journalist's name which is credited on an article.

Case study
When journalists ask for case studies they are looking for people to write about as a main part of their article, providing details of their individual situation and how a particular issue has affected them. They will go into depth in the piece much more than an anecdote.

Conflict of Interest
This is really important. It is where you have competing interests. If you are likely to receive personal benefit from doing something without declaring it, that would be a conflict of interest. Sometimes even declaring it would not be enough. For example, I do not take payment for endorsing products. As a consumer champion I have to remain independent and people would not trust me to give an independent opinion on a company if it were also paying me to say nice things.

Contributor
You will be a contributor if you give some information for an outlet to use on TV, radio, online or in print.

Copy
The text in an article or on screen.

Credits
Acknowledgement of your contribution. If you give an expert opinion, for example, you will be credited with your name and maybe your business, if applicable.

Crew
The production team and everyone working behind the camera.

Correspondent
A journalist working from a particular location to report on the news from there. For example, "Paris Correspondent".

Glossary

Deadline

If a journalist gives you a date and time by which they need a quote, picture or information etc. then you must ensure they receive this by the deadline. If you don't then you risk that journalist never using you again and your PR not being included.

Director

Their role can be varied. Often responsible for ensuring the producer's vision is realised, leading the crew they also direct presenters, contributors and work with the editor on the final product. The director is responsible for what goes on in front of the camera.

Editor

For online and print this person will adapt the piece, changing parts to fit with the outlet's style, correcting grammar and cutting words, lines and paragraphs, where necessary.

For TV and radio, the editor puts the **Rushes** (see below) together in order, making decisions on what is kept and what remains "on the cutting room floor".

Expenses

If you incur costs, such as travel, then these would be expenses that are usually paid for by the media company.

Expert

Definitions of this word vary! Usually considered to be someone who has a specialism and lots of knowledge in one particular area. Another popular definition is someone who knows more about something in an average room.

Feature article

Non-fiction, non-news, it is usually a human interest story, and may be an opinion piece.

First-person piece

A feature which is written by a journalist/writer about themselves—or ghost-written by a journalist on behalf of someone else.

Floor Manager

Responsible for people and equipment in the studio. They ensure that filming goes to plan, live or recorded, and that everyone knows what they are doing.

Interview

This will be a structured conversation where the journalist, reporter or presenter will ask you questions on the agreed topic.

Magazine programme

These contain various segments throughout the programme, such as features, interviews, clips, discussions. BBC's *The One Show* and *This Morning* on ITV are current examples of UK magazine programmes.

News article

A topical piece discussing a subject in the news for which you may be asked to provide comment/opinion.

Opinion piece

First person article giving a strong opinion on a particular topic.

Presenter

The person who introduces and fronts a radio or TV programme.

Producer

There are a number of different producer roles. For example, the executive producer, who supervises the producers and is often the head of a production company, the edit producer who works with the editor, line producer who is responsible for the logistics, such as health and safety and budgeting.

The producer you are most likely to come into contact with is responsible for what goes on behind the camera. They have the job of coming up with ideas and booking guests or overseeing one part of the programme. One magazine programme may have several producers, each choosing one guest for the episode. It might be a producer who books you and has a discussion with you about appearing on a show and/or may pass you to a researcher to find out more.

Production Company

Produces radio, TV and big screen content. Whilst many TV outlets do have some programmes made in house they are mostly made by production companies which have pitched an idea to the outlet commissioners.

Reporter

Keeps viewers/listeners updated with analysis on news.

Researcher

Undertakes investigation of topics and often finds the experts to speak about them.

Runner

Undertakes the basic tasks for the crew and people in front of the camera.

Rushes

The raw video recordings taken straight from the video camera before they reach the editor.

Script

Even with factual programmes there is usually a script. This is particularly used with live TV to help with timings and to control what is being said. Don't worry if you are on to answer questions/provide expertise, you won't have to learn a script. However, you should be equipped with the questions and your likely answers, so that there aren't any big surprises for anyone involved in making the programme!

Slot

The start/end time for which a programme is scheduled.

Statement

An official comment on a subject. For example, if there is an item in the news about a company, they might be asked to provide a comment. "A spokesperson for x company said…" is an example.

Syndication

Where an article that has already been published is then republished in another publication.

Talking head

A journalist, presenter or guest talking directly to camera, where just the head and shoulders are shown.

Tip-off fee

If you provide a story idea or propose a case study to an editor, you may get a referral fee or 'tip-off fee'.

Vox pop

Abbreviated from the Latin *vox populi* (voice of the people), this is a style of interview featuring members of the public speaking to an interviewer or presenter. For example, a person stopped in the street and asked to give their opinion on a subject in the news.

Word count

Let's end on the thing I find most difficult! You'll sometimes be given a word count if you are providing more than a quick comment or if you are writing an article. You'll be given a minimum and maximum within which to write. I struggle with the maximum, as I always have so much to say!

References

Introduction

The Complaining Cow website **https://thecomplainingcow.co.uk/**

CHAPTER 1: **Starting to get publicity**

2 Get your mindset in a good place

Tigz Rice photography **https://www.tigzrice.com/**

The Naked Podcast Tigz Rice **https://www.bbc.co.uk/programmes/p08jy56l**

6 Local online Press

Janine McDonald, founder of Clear the Clutter Now
https://clearthecluttternow.co.uk/

Clear the Clutter Now: Streamline Your Life by doing Just 3 Things
https://amzn.to/44Xa8Qj

7 Contact your local radio station

Rhiannon Abbott is the owner of The Epsom Bakehouse
https://theepsombakehouse.co.uk/

8. Invite the press to events

Diane Ivory, founder of Forensic Minds **https://forensicminds.co.uk/**

9. Local free advertising

Linda Gransby, founder of Memories and Photos
https://memoriesandphotos.co.uk/

10. Present local/community radio

The Complaining Cow Consumer Show on East London radio,
https://thecomplainingcow.co.uk/complaining-cow-consumer-show/

11. #JournoRequest

Dr Clair Burley, Chartered Clinical Psychologist **https://drclair.com/**

The Independent "How to break up with someone the right way"
https://www.independent.co.uk/life-style/break-up-right-way-b1840186.html

The Independent "How to make a long distance relationship work"
https://www.independent.co.uk/life-style/love-sex/long-distance-relationship-tips-advice-love-how-b1875582.html

Style magazine "How to make friends as an adult: your guide to finding new mates at the gym" **https://www.stylist.co.uk/fitness-health/wellbeing/tired-of-being-a-fitness-lone-wolf-heres-how-to-make-friends-at-the-gym/591615**

Elle "Why are onscreen love triangles so compelling?"
https://www.elle.com/uk/life-and-culture/culture/a40958572/why-are-onscreen-love-triangles-so-compelling/

12. #JournoRequest Case study request group

#JournoRequest Case study request group
https://www.facebook.com/groups/648486041940845

14. Press Plugs

Press Plugs **https://pressplugs.co.uk/trial/**

References

15 Check Instagram

Linda Scerri runs Save Money Make Money
https://www.facebook.com/groups/savemoneymakemoney

16 Editorielle

Editorielle **https://www.editorielle.com**

Roxy King-Clark, coach **https://roxyking.coach/**

Metro article "Masks, vaccines and mental health: How Covid has shaped the world" **https://metro.co.uk/2022/02/05/in-focus-how-covid-has-shaped-the-world-16041592/**

17 Dot Star Media

Dot Star Media **https://dotstar.media/**

18 Research the outlet

Readly **https://gb.readly.com/**

PressReader **https://www.pressreader.com/**

19 Look at frequency

Joe Nutkins, Dog Training for Essex & Suffolk centre **https://dogtrainingessex-suffolk.co.uk/**

Senior Dogs **https://issuu.com/mousemediastudio/docs/winter**

21 Research journalists and think about whether to typecast them

Metro article "Single mum's lockdown business coaching people on LinkedIn lets her ditch renting to buy her first home" **https://metro.co.uk/2022/06/25/single-mums-lockdown-business-lets-her-ditch-renting-to-buy-first-home-16890338/**

Metro article "Pastime to full-time: How the pandemic made us turn our hobbies into main jobs" **https://metro.co.uk/2022/07/17/pastime-to-full-time-how-the-pandemic-turned-our-hobbies-into-jobs-16950517/**

23 Response Source

Response Source **https://www.responsesource.com/freetrial/**

Dalia Hawley, founder of Dalia Botanique **https://daliabotanique.co.uk/**

24 Go international

Help a Reporter Out **https://www.helpareporter.com/**

SourceBottle **https://www.sourcebottle.com/**

Qwoted **https://app.qwoted.com/**

Mangla Sachdev founder of Business in a Bag
https://www.instagram.com/expatbusinessinabag/

25 Facebook Lightbulb group

Facebook Lightbulb **https://www.facebook.com/groups/lightbulbhangout**

27 Feature Me

Feature Me! UK **https://www.facebook.com/groups/166398616795827**

Boots "I do Christmas my way" **https://www.boots.com/inspiration-advice/wellness-advice/life-balance/wellbeing-advice/christmas-my-way**

28 Make The Headlines

Make The Headlines website **https://www.maketheheadlines.co.uk/**

Make the Headlines Instagram
https://www.instagram.com/maketheheadlines.co.uk/

32 Sell your story direct to specific outlets

The Sun Sell Your Story **https://www.thesun.co.uk/sell-your-story-sun/**

Mirror Got a Story? **https://www.mirror.co.uk/got-a-story/**

37 Don't always expect hyperlinks

Lizzie Cernik **https://www.theguardian.com/profile/lizzie-cernik**

44 Try a cheeky request or stunt

Lisa Johnson, Business Strategist **https://www.lisajohnson.com/**

45 Media Matchmaker

Media Matchmaker **https://mediamatchmaker.co.uk/**

Free two week trial **https://mediamatchmaker.co.uk/freecow/**

World Jenny's Day **https://worldjennysday.com/**

OK! Magazine online **https://www.ok.co.uk/lifestyle/the-last-conversation-16-year-25111149?fbclid=IwAR1t_J6uPATSd3wKXVs2pvj0Puex2CW6i0LrjfPlSv1C3PAb6uRRTblfl1w**

46 Talent Talks

Talent Talks **www.talenttalks.co.uk**

47 Unicorn Casting

Unicorn Casting **https://www.instagram.com/castingunicorn/**

48 Triangle News

Triangle News **https://trianglenews.co.uk/**

49 Write a book

How to Complain: The Essential Consumer Guide to Getting Refunds, Redress and Results! **https://thecomplainingcow.co.uk/product/how-to-complain-the-essential-consumer-guide-to-getting-refunds-redress-and-results/**

101 Habits of an Effective Complainer **https://thecomplainingcow.co.uk/product/101-habits-of-an-effective-complainer/**

Reedsy Blog **https://blog.reedsy.com/writers-resources/**

50 Don't get concerned about "vanity publishing"

Make Money Online **https://amzn.to/4a2wfpQ**

51 Get in someone else's book

Paul Lewis *Money Box: Your toolkit for balancing your budget, growing your bank balance and living a better financial life* **https://amzn.to/4bzXmcW**

Caroline Bramwell **https://www.linkedin.com/in/carolinebramwell/**
Fearless: Adventures with Extraordinary Women **https://amzn.to/4bN6LOc**

52 Collaborate on a book

Lisa Williams, Vision Board Coach **https://www.lisawilliams-lmg.co.uk/**
Seen **https://amzn.to/4ayPM0J**

"Rhyl businesswoman shares story of miscarriages to inspire others 'in darkness'" **https://www.rhyljournal.co.uk/news/19635223.rhyl-businesswoman-shares-story-miscarriages-inspire-others-in-darkness/**

53 Keep up to date with current thinking

Her Own Space **https://www.herownspace.com/**

55 Could a customer have a story?

Nicola Toner, a Crowdfunding mentor
https://nicolatoner.com/crowdfunding-mentor

The Red Lion **https://www.theredlionhollington.co.uk/**

Crowdfunding to prevent it being sold to someone else
https://www.crowdfunder.co.uk/p/make-the-red-lion-hollington-independent

"Landlord needs £50k more to save village pub from being sold off"
https://www.derbytelegraph.co.uk/whats-on/food-drink/landlord-needs-50k-more-save-7744056

"Follow Meet Red Lion licensee who has bought his pub after 10 years"
https://www.derbytelegraph.co.uk/whats-on/food-drink/meet-red-lion-licensee-who-8241172.amp

56 Use Medium to publish articles

Medium **https://medium.com/**

57 Pitch to *Authority Magazine*

Authority Magazine **https://medium.com/authority-magazine/ongoing-interview-series-in-authority-magazine-7d633a349753**

59 Use your vulnerabilities

Maddy Alexander-Grout, founder of Mad About Money **https://madaboutmoneyofficial.co.uk/**

"My spending addiction left me £40k in debt" **https://uk.style.yahoo.com/style/my-spending-addiction-left-me-40k-in-debt-125732766.html**

Dr Marianne Trent, a Clinical Psychologist **https://www.goodthinkingpsychology.co.uk/**

Author **https://amzn.to/3UVhHSZ**

The Aspiring Psychologist Podcast **https://podcasts.apple.com/gb/podcast/the-aspiring-psychologist-podcast/id1605628278**

60 Be controversial in mainstream media

Samantha Jayne, Spiritual Coach **https://samantha-jayne.co.uk/**

"Why I'll never date a man who is paid less than me" **https://www.dailymail.co.uk/femail/relationships/article-12017077/Why-Ill-NEVER-date-man-earns-me.html**

61 Consider your brand

Lightbulb **https://www.facebook.com/groups/lightbulbhangout**

63 Get reviews from customers

VideoAsk **https://www.videoask.com/**

Georgina L Nestor, copywriter and coach **https://www.fearlesswords.co.uk/**

64 Get reviews from people in the media

The Complaining Cow media page **https://thecomplainingcow.co.uk/media/**

65 Keep things simple

Continuing of work on reporting on ADR https://thecomplainingcow.co.uk/adr-all-about-it-for-world-ombudsman-day/

66 Send gifts

Julie Čolan, founder of Secret Whispers https://www.secretwhispers.co.uk/

67 Work on your SEO

Semrush https://www.semrush.com/

SheerSEO https://www.sheerseo.com/

Wincher https://www.wincher.com/

Google Analytics https://marketingplatform.google.com/intl/en_uk/about/analytics/

71 Don't worry if you have nothing to sell

BBC Radio 5 phone in https://youtu.be/yiVoH-zsD8U

BBC Breakfast https://youtu.be/-kmq-iSDKNk

74 Network

Kerry Hales, Kerry Hales Coaching https://www.kerryhales.com/

Life from the knicker drawer https://amzn.to/48xuT5P

78 Recommend other experts

Jasmine Birtles https://www.jasminebirtles.com/

"Jasmine Birtles explains interest, inflation & stagnation" https://thecomplainingcow.co.uk/jasmine-birtles-explains-interest-inflation-stagnation/

References

82 Get your images used

Press Loft **https://www.pressloft.com/**

Susan Bonnar, founder of The British Craft House
https://thebritishcrafthouse.co.uk/

83 Set up Google Alerts for your name and keywords

Google alerts **https://www.google.co.uk/alerts**

Talkwalker **https://www.talkwalker.com/alerts**

84 Help people out!

"Mum who was switched to prepay energy meter without being told wins £620 in compensation" **https://www.mirror.co.uk/money/mum-who-switched-prepay-energy-29027595**

85 Give great customer service!

"5 ways to get rave reviews and referrals"
https://thecomplainingcow.co.uk/customer-service-freebie/

86 Awareness Days

AwarenessDays.com **https://www.awarenessdays.com/awareness-days-calendar/category/uk-awareness-day/**

Stacey Brown founder of Lucky Penny Creations
https://www.facebook.com/LuckyPennyCreations/

Hear us Roar: 12 Women's Journeys with Endometriosis raising awareness— supporting women **https://amzn.to/43h1ew0**

90 Think of a journey

"Single mum's lockdown business coaching people on LinkedIn lets her ditch renting to buy her first home" **https://metro.co.uk/2022/06/25/single-mums-lockdown-business-lets-her-ditch-renting-to-buy-first-home-16890338/**

CHAPTER 2: Prepare for your coverage

A phone-in on *BBC Radio 5*
https://youtu.be/yiVoH-zsD8U?si=t_6k1BKB1UIsomKI

103 Think about what clothes you will wear!

Lindsay Edwards, personal stylist **https://www.lindsayedwardsstylist.com/**

108 But don't over prepare!

Jenny Leggott, founder of Sammy Rambles **https://www.sammyrambles.co.uk/** and Dragonball **https://www.dragonball.uk.com/**

Numerous books **https://amzn.to/3Khx4QL**

CHAPTER 3: At the event

129 Always be aware!

'Resting bitch face' 3 full seconds on *BBC Breakfast*! **https://youtu.be/AF0qXdcv2vo?si=Sf_nWdspBj15qWbH**

130 Being controversial on air

Anupa Roper, Body Image Educator and bestselling Children's Author **https://sparrowlegs.com/**

Sparrowlegs **https://amzn.to/3WUw4JT**

"Activist calls for 'fat shaming' to be made a crime as debate erupts over free speech" **https://www.express.co.uk/news/uk/1510800/tilly-ramsay-steve-allen-fat-shaming-apology-talkradio**

132 Give the presenter a product

The One Show segment
https://youtu.be/XgEEZ27egPA?si=4m0p0dDX9G0_rhU-

134 Wear Different clothes

Showreel https://www.youtube.com/watch?v=Tu24ioaD_Jg

137 Don't give out business cards!

Marta Zaczkowska, Waxing Expert https://waxingspecialist.co.uk/

139 Don't worry about being cut!

"Glasgow Willy Wonka experience—what happened" https://thecomplainingcow.co.uk/glasgow-willy-wonka-experience-what-happened/

CHAPTER 4: Getting paid

144 Agents

Showreel https://youtu.be/Tu24ioaD_Jg?si=2QnSk76w6kO5QILF

Tom Stanhope, a professional video producer
https://www.linkedin.com/in/tomstanhope/

Maddy Alexander-Grout TikTok Account
https://www.tiktok.com/@madaboutmoneyofficial

CHAPTER 5: After your appearances

Facebook Lightbulb https://www.facebook.com/groups/lightbulbhangout

146 Follow up appearances on social media

Sky News article "What's happening with Etsy and its reserve system?" https://news.sky.com/story/could-etsy-sellers-boycott-the-platform-because-of-its-reserve-system-12931828

Press release "Etsy hassles—UK company offers an alternative for makers and crafters" https://thecomplainingcow.co.uk/etsy-hassles-uk-company-offers-an-alternative-for-makers-and-crafters/

Interview on *The Complaining Cow Consumer Show*
https://thecomplainingcow.co.uk/founder-of-the-british-craft-house-on-the-etsy-fightback/

154 Ignore the trolls on online articles

"As Sainsbury's turns away a guide dog, the CONSUMER FIGHTBACK column reveals your rights under the Equality Act" **https://www.thisismoney.co.uk/money/experts/article-7857521/Sainsburys-turns-away-guide-dog-Equality-Act-rights.html**

155 Ignore the trolls on social media too

Lisa Johnson's podcast *How To Deal With People Who Treat you Badly Online* **https://podcasts.apple.com/gb/podcast/making-money-online-with-lisa-johnson/id1577338091**

Kate Hall, Founder of The Full Freezer **https://www.thefullfreezer.com/**

Books **https://amzn.to/3KhmbOX**

Instagram reel **https://www.instagram.com/reel/CPJDyD6nyn4/?utm_source=ig_web_copy_link**

Chrissy Teigen when she apologised for online bullying **https://www.bbc.co.uk/news/entertainment-arts-57478066**

156 Be prepared to not be fully happy!

Judi Hampton, founder of Look See & Feel Amazing **https://lookseeandfeelamazing.com/**

Dr Marianne Trent, Clinical Psychologist **https://www.goodthinkingpsychology.co.uk/**

159 Laugh if things go wrong and use to your advantage

First TikTok **https://www.tiktok.com/@thecomplainingcow/video/7344629480352206113**

CHAPTER 6: Building your media contact list

165 Build a press release list

General Data Protection Regulations (GDPRs)
https://www.gov.uk/data-protection

Information Commissioner's Office
https://ico.org.uk/for-organisations/data-protection-fee/

166 Watch journalist movements

CISION Sector Digest https://www.cision.co.uk/lp/sector-digests/

CHAPTER 7: Sending out press releases

179 Do your due diligence

Blog post "Insensitive language forces Boots signage change"
https://thecomplainingcow.co.uk/insensitive-language-forces-boots-signage-change/

Kekezza Reece https://www.krcoaching.co.uk/

182 Check out local news publishing sites

Press release *London Daily News* https://www.londondaily.news/judge-rinder-and-abba-voyage-inspire-heathcote-pupils-during-national-careers-week/

183 Sell your story to a news agency

Jam Press https://www.jampress.co.uk/

Caters Media Group https://catersmediagroup.com/

184 Get on distribution lists

Mr Pothole **https://www.facebook.com/mrpotholeuk**

BBC Breakfast **https://youtu.be/_06VFXUVnnc?si=giuYy82y_zORxciQ**

185 Collaborate

Article in *Financial Times* "Money saving travel tips to lift the gloom of 'Blue Monday'"
https://www.ft.com/content/0edc8550-f786-11e7-88f7-5465a6ce1a00

195 Keep an eye out for relevant issues

Press release **https://thecomplainingcow.co.uk/caa-launches-consultation-and-tells-no-one/**

Story coverage *This Is Money* **https://www.thisismoney.co.uk/money/holidays/article-8834365/Airline-regulator-slammed-botching-customer-complaints-review.html**

196 Tipoffs

"BA flies into customer relations disaster"
https://www.ft.com/content/e3ebfd6e-469e-11e7-8519-9f94ee97d996

201 Promote products appropriately

The Grief Collective: Stories of Life, Loss & Learning to Heal
https://amzn.to/3RYi1yK

203 Newsjack

Article *This is Money* "Most complained-about broadband, TV and phone firms revealed" **https://www.thisismoney.co.uk/money/bills/article-11679177/Which-broadband-TV-phone-firms-complaints-Ofgem-reveals-figures.html**

205 Press release distribution services

Slashdot **https://slashdot.org/software/press-release-distribution/free-trial/**

References

206 Put your press release on your website

Canva **https://www.canva.com/**

"Looking a gift card in the mouth"
https://thecomplainingcow.co.uk/looking-a-gift-card-in-the-mouth/

The One Show **https://youtu.be/XgEEZ27egPA**

CHAPTER 8: Boost your profile outside of traditional media

212 Be active on Facebook

Delegate Wranglers
https://www.facebook.com/groups/TheDelegateWranglers

213 Run a competition

Zaria Sleith **https://www.facebook.com/BrandingbyZaria/**

Facebook Pages, groups and events
https://www.facebook.com/policies_center/pages_groups_events?_

Types of lottery you can run without a licence
https://www.gamblingcommission.gov.uk/public-and-players/guide/page/types-of-lottery-you-can-run-without-a-licence

215 Put your freebie link on your cover photo on Facebook

Facebook cover picture **https://www.facebook.com/helen.dewdney.9/**

216 Start a YouTube channel

The Complaining Cow YouTube channel
https://www.youtube.com/c/HelenDewdney

219 Involve your MP!

First meeting with Iain Duncan Smith **https://thecomplainingcow.co.uk/the-complaining-cow-meets-iain-duncan-smith-idsfail/**

Second meeting with Ian Duncan Smith **https://www.thecomplainingcow.co.uk/round-2-the-complaining-cow-meets-ids/**

YouTube channel **https://www.youtube.com/@HelenDewdney/videos**

220 Build relationships with big businesses

"Case Study: Tesco and a Consumer Champion" **https://thecomplainingcow.co.uk/case-study-tesco-and-a-consumer-champion/**

To contact CEOs **https://www.ceoemail.com/**

221 Contact bloggers

UK Money Bloggers **https://ukmoneybloggers.com/work-with-us/**

222 Podcasts

Podcast Connection
https://www.facebook.com/groups/podcastguestconnection

Podcast Guest Collaboration
https://www.facebook.com/groups/podcastguestcollaboration

Business GROWTH Opportunities Through GUEST Appearances
https://www.facebook.com/groups/businessgrowthviaguestopportunities/

Star Projects **https://www.starprojects.london/about**

Bust and Beyond **https://podcasts.apple.com/gb/podcast/e11julia-starzyk/id1648130007?i=1000604926041**

223 Podmatch

Podmatch **https://podmatch.com/**

224 MatchMaker.fm

MatchMaker.fm **https://www.matchmaker.fm/home**

227 Set up your own podcast

Aspiring Psychologist podcast
https://www.goodthinkingpsychology.co.uk/podcast

228 Reach out to influencers

Le Tricoteur **https://letricoteur.co/products/womens-aran-navy-off-the-shoulder-guernsey-jumper**

Erica Kim **https://www.instagram.com/ahistoryofarchitecture/**

229 Join influencer marketing Facebook groups

UK Influencer Opportunities
https://www.facebook.com/groups/UKBloggerOpportunities

231 Do your own videos

Helen Dewdney YouTube channel **https://www.youtube.com/HelenDewdney**

TikTok **https://www.tiktok.com/@thecomplainingcow**

Instagram **https://www.instagram.com/thecomplainingcow/**

Jenny Leggott, founder of Sammy Rambles **https://www.sammyrambles.co.uk/** and Dragonball **https://www.dragonball.uk.com/**

Tom Stanhope, a professional video producer
https://www.linkedin.com/in/tomstanhope/

232 Join Grow Your Business with Video group on Facebook

Grow Your Business with Video Grow Your Business with Video
https://www.facebook.com/groups/growabusinesswithvideo

233 Do videos for other people

Helen Dewdney storytelling channel
https://www.youtube.com/@helendewdneythecomplaining3499

237 If you don't ask, you don't get

How to Complain: The Essential Consumer Guide for Getting Refunds, Redress and Results! **https://thecomplainingcow.co.uk/product/how-to-complain-the-essential-consumer-guide-to-getting-refunds-redress-and-results/**

101 Habits of an Effective Complainer **https://thecomplainingcow.co.uk/101-habits-of-an-effective-complainer-new-consumer-guide/**

Rob Rinder videoed testimonial
https://youtu.be/faKXyoadXgU?si=Ed1_A8YLRoeYtFlB

238 Practice on social media posts

Helen (Pritchard) Tudor LinkedIn
https://www.linkedin.com/in/helenpritchard/

Lea Turner LinkedIn **https://www.linkedin.com/in/lea-turner/**

Lisa Johnson, Business Strategist **https://www.lisajohnson.com/**

239 Be controversial on social media

Mad About Money **https://madaboutmoneyofficial.co.uk/**

Daily Mail "Mother discovers clever hack for getting a McDonald's burger and fries for just £1.99" **https://www.dailymail.co.uk/femail/article-11598785/How-McDonalds-burger-fries-just-1-99.html**

240 Try a Q and A or free webinar

James Bore, Bores Group **https://www.bores.com/**

245 Speaking at small events

4Networking **https://4nonline.biz/**

247 Sign up to speaking agencies

Speakerhub **https://speakerhub.com/**

Speakernet **https://speakernet.co.uk/**

References

International Women's Day
https://www.internationalwomensday.com/Speakers

248 Plan your presentation effectively

Penny Haslam's book *Make Yourself a Little Bit Famous*
https://amzn.to/3rkbDbj

250 Offer a discount

The Express "I'm proof it pays to complain, says woman who sued Tesco and WON" **https://www.express.co.uk/finance/personalfinance/556367/Complaining-Cow-author-gives-advice-for-customer-satisfaction**

The Complaining Cow Consumer Show
https://thecomplainingcow.co.uk/complaining-cow-consumer-show/

252 Google listing

Google business listing **https://www.google.com/intl/en_uk/business/** to set it up.

253 Awards

Corporate awards: Buyer beware!
https://www.thecomplainingcow.co.uk/corporate-awards-buyer-beware/

CHAPTER 9: Write yourself and get your name out there

Financial Times "Avoid a holiday hire car nightmare"
https://www.ft.com/content/a34469fe-4ee0-11e8-ac41-759eee1efb74

Ombudsman Omnishambles
https://thecomplainingcow.co.uk/ombudsman-omnishambles-new-report-exposes-serious-failings-in-ombudsman-approval-and-oversight/

More Ombudsman Omnishambles **https://ceoemail.com/oo2final.pdf**

This is Money Consumer Fightback column
https://www.thisismoney.co.uk/home/search.html?s=&authornamef=Helen+Dewdney+For+This+Is+Money

255 Pitch to editors

Maddy Alexander-Grout, founder of Mad About Money
https://madaboutmoneyofficial.co.uk/

Maddy in *The Sun* https://www.thesun.co.uk/?s=maddy+alexander-grout

256 Journo Resources

Journo Resources **https://www.journoresources.org.uk/**

257 Write at Home

Write at Home **https://writeathome.beehiiv.com/**

258 Journo Resources Substack

Weekly free newsletter **https://journoresources.substack.com/**

259 Freelance Writing Jobs

Freelance Writing Jobs **https://freelancewritingjobs.substack.com/**

261 Get free expert help with pitching your writing

Facebook group Succeed in Freelance Journalism
https://www.facebook.com/groups/succeedinfreelancejournalism

269 Use the content for a blog post

Blog post "All you need to know about secondary tickets and touts"
https://thecomplainingcow.co.uk/all-you-need-to-know-about-secondary-tickets-and-touts/

CHAPTER 10: Performing at your best so you are asked back!

275 **Get a showreel made**

Second showreel **https://youtu.be/DyYDJHznYtQ?si=Inir3z8_GIBIJNu8**

Third showreel **https://youtu.be/Tu24ioaD_Jg?si=UOi_FUCIEIBdORwu**

279 **Contact me!**

Commissions **https://thecomplainingcow.co.uk/commissions/**

The Complaining Cow website **https://thecomplainingcow.co.uk/**

Acknowledgements

As always, thanks first and foremost to my long-suffering friend, mentor and editor Marcus Williamson for the suggestions, the editing of what seemed like hundreds of versions and proof reading. We finally got to the publishing stage, hurrah!

Thank you to all the journalists for their contributions.

Thank you to the numerous business people who have shared their examples of how these tips worked for them in getting free PR.

Thank you to everyone who has written testimonials for my work, booked me and given support through sharing social media posts and recommendations.

And, of course, to my dear husband Tony, who puts up with all this nonsense, and to my son Ollie, who has no interest whatsoever in anything 'media' and keeps me firmly grounded!

Printed in Great Britain
by Amazon